Project Management Institute

Practice Standard for
Work Breakdown Structures

Project Management Institute

Practice Standard for
Work Breakdown Structures

Project Management Institute

Newtown Square, Pennsylvania USA

Library of Congress Cataloging-in-Publication Data

Project Management Institute practice standard for work breakdown structures
         p. cm.
     Includes bibliographical references and index.
     ISBN 1-880410-81-8
        1. Project management.   I. Project Management Institute.   II. Title: Practice
standard for work breakdown structures.
     HD69.P75P76168   2001
     658.4'04—dc21   2001048475

ISBN: 1-880410-81-8

Published by: Project Management Institute, Inc.
             Four Campus Boulevard
             Newtown Square, Pennsylvania 19073-3299 USA
             Phone: 610-356-4600 or Visit our website: www.pmi.org
             E-mail: pmihq@pmi.org

10   9   8   7   6   5   4   3   2

Contents

List of Figures

Foreword

On behalf of the Project Management Institute (PMI®) Board of Directors, I am pleased to present PMI's first practice standard, the *Project Management Institute Practice Standard for Work Breakdown Structures*.

The *Project Management Institute Practice Standard for Work Breakdown Structures* is an important step in PMI's continuing commitment to define the body of knowledge supporting the project management profession, and to develop standards for its application. The dedicated volunteers who worked on PMI's Ethics, Standards, and Accreditation (ESA) Project first distilled the Project Management Body of Knowledge (PMBOK®) in 1983. Building on that work, PMI published the *PMBOK® Standards* in 1987.

The publication of *A Guide to the Project Management Body of Knowledge* (*PMBOK® Guide*) – 1996 Edition continued the evolution. Today the *PMBOK® Guide* – 2000 Edition is an *American National Standard* and the *de facto* global standard for project management.

It has been PMI's intent for many years to supplement the information in the *PMBOK® Guide* by providing both industry-specific extensions and practice standards that guide the practice of the profession through more in-depth information on the listed inputs, tools and techniques, and outputs. The *Project Management Institute Practice Standard for Work Breakdown Structures* is the first such practice standard. It provides guidance in the initial generation, subsequent development, and application of the Work Breakdown Structure.

Finally, I would like to thank the project team, led by Kim Colenso, who worked so diligently to bring this standard to fruition. Dedicated and competent volunteers have always been the backbone of PMI's success, and this publication is yet another example.

Hugh Woodward

Hugh Woodward, PMP
Chair – PMI Board of Directors

Preface

This *Project Management Institute Practice Standard for Work Breakdown Structures* provides guidance in the initial generation, subsequent development, and application of the Work Breakdown Structure (WBS). The target audience for this standard includes project managers, project team members, contract personnel, and others who participate or have an interest in any aspect of the management of projects. In using this *Practice Standard*, it must be recognized that as projects vary, so may the resulting WBSs. There are, however, certain universal principles that this *Practice Standard* addresses.

The *Project Management Institute Practice Standard for Work Breakdown Structures* is consistent with the current release of *A Guide to the Project Management Body of Knowledge* (*PMBOK® Guide*) – 2000 Edition. The *Practice Standard* also includes information derived from accepted project management industry sources. The Project Management Institute Standards Program will periodically update the *Project Management Institute Practice Standard for Work Breakdown Structures* as part of the planned evolution of the standards documents. Your comments are both requested and welcome.

The *Project Management Institute Practice Standard for Work Breakdown Structures* is organized as follows:

Introduction	Introduces the WBS concept.
What Is a WBS?	Defines the WBS and its characteristics.
Why Use a WBS?	Defines the benefits derived from using a WBS.
How to Create a WBS?	Documents the steps required for building a WBS and presents guidelines for determining if the WBS is sufficient for subsequent planning and control.
Appendix A–D	Provides background information on the Project Management Institute Standards Program and the *Project Management Institute Practice Standard for Work Breakdown Structures* project.
Appendix E–O	Provides documented industry examples to aid the reader in further understanding, creating, and using WBSs. Each appendix represents an approach tailored to a specific purpose, application, or industry. Examples are in different stages of completion and represent the evolutionary development of a WBS. None of the examples should be taken as the only *right* WBS for that type of project.
References	Offers literary support for the information contained in the *Project Management Institute Practice Standard for Work Breakdown Structures*.
Glossary	Provides clarification of key terms that exist in the project management profession, including those that have subtle or variable meanings depending on the organization and industry.

Chapter 1

Introduction

1.1 CONCEPT

Successful project management uses planning techniques to define the project objectives in sufficient detail to support effective management of the project. The *Work Breakdown Structure* (WBS) provides the foundation for defining work as it relates to project objectives and establishes the structure for managing the work to its completion.

The WBS is used in projects to define:

- The project's work in terms of *deliverables* and further *decomposition* of these deliverables into components. Depending on the decomposition method used, it may also define the project's life-cycle process in terms of process deliverables appropriate to that project and organization.

And is the basis for establishing:

- All the effort/cost to be expended on supporting processes and the creation of the deliverables
- The assigned responsibility for accomplishing and coordinating the work.

As a definition for use within this *Project Management Institute Practice Standard for Work Breakdown Structures*, a project can be internally focused, externally focused, or both. Deliverables for these projects can take the form of products and/or services.

Internally focused projects may produce deliverables as inputs to other project steps, other individuals, or for organizations within a company. Externally focused projects typically produce outputs and deliverables to people or organizations outside the company, such as *customers* or project sponsors. Many projects produce both internally and externally focused deliverables. A WBS should be routinely prepared in all cases.

Developing a WBS is an essential step during the initial *phases* of a project—as soon as the basic *scope* has been identified. The initial WBS may be created with limited scope information. However, it will require rework as additional scope information is developed or made available by more complete analysis of the project work to be performed.

This *Practice Standard* provides insight into WBS development and application. It has been prepared as a guide and should be used accordingly. It is expected that use of the principles found in this standard will enable the user to prepare a useful and high-quality WBS.

1.2 OBJECTIVE

The primary objectives of the *Project Management Institute Practice Standard for Work Breakdown Structures* are to provide a common ground for understanding the concepts and benefits of the WBS, and to present a standard application of the WBS as a project management tool. The intent is to encourage the consistent development of the WBS as a project management tool and, as a result, improve the planning and control of projects.

Chapter 2

What Is a Work Breakdown Structure?

2.1 COMMON USAGE OF TERMS

The following commonly used words have generally accepted meanings:

Work Sustained physical or mental effort to overcome obstacles and achieve an objective or result; a specific *activity*, duty, function, or assignment often being a part or phase of some larger undertaking; something produced or accomplished by effort, exertion, or exercise of skill.

Breakdown To divide into parts or categories; to separate into simpler substances; to undergo decomposition.

Structure Something arranged in a definite pattern of organization.

These definitions imply that a Work Breakdown Structure (WBS) has the following characteristics:

- It is representative of work as an activity, and this work has a tangible result.
- It is arranged in a hierarchical structure.
- It has an objective or tangible result, which is referred to as a deliverable.

A WBS, as defined in the *PMBOK® Guide* – 2000 Edition, is:

> A deliverable-oriented grouping of project elements that organizes and defines the total work scope of the project. Each descending level represents an increasingly detailed definition of the project work (Project Management Institute 2000).

2.2 CONCEPT

2.2.1 Overview

The *WBS elements* assist the project *stakeholders* in developing a clear vision of an end product of the project and of the overall process by which it will be created. The WBS divides the project scope into hierarchal, manageable, definable packages of work that balance the control needs of management with an appropriate and effective level of project data. The various levels of the WBS aid in focusing communication with stakeholders and clearly identifying accountability to the level of detail required for managing and controlling the project.

The upper levels of the WBS typically reflect the major deliverable work areas of the project or phases in the project's life cycle. These levels also provide logical summary points for assessing performance accomplishments, as well as measuring cost and schedule performance. The content of the upper levels varies depending upon the type of project and the industry in which it resides. Therefore, to avoid confusion and rework, it is often prudent to consider defining the labels for the different levels of the WBS prior to its construction. The lower WBS elements provide appropriate focus for scope, cost, and schedule development.

Whenever work is structured, easily identifiable, and clearly within the capabilities of individuals, project stakeholders can confidently expect the objectives associated with that work can—and will—be achieved.

2.2.2 WBS Overview: Deliverables

A deliverable, as defined in the *PMBOK® Guide* – 2000 Edition, is:

> Any measurable, tangible, verifiable outcome, result, or item that must be produced to complete a project or part of a project. Often used more narrowly in reference to an external deliverable, which is a deliverable that is subject to approval by the project sponsor or customer (Project Management Institute 2000).

As an integral concept in the definition of a WBS, it is important to understand the broad context of a deliverable as noted in the *PMBOK® Guide* and how a WBS can be used in that broad context. In addition, the WBS provides the foundation for subsequently integrating the *work package* details and deliverables with all other aspects of project initiating, planning, executing, controlling, and closing.

A work package, as defined in the *PMBOK® Guide* – 2000 Edition, is:

> A deliverable at the lowest level of the work breakdown structure, when that deliverable may be assigned to another project manager to plan and execute. This may be accomplished through the use of a subproject where the work package may be further decomposed into activities (Project Management Institute 2000).

2.2.3 WBS Overview: Design

A well-developed WBS that presents information at the appropriate level of detail and in formats and structures meaningful to those performing the work is an invaluable tool in project management.

The WBS:

- Decomposes (or disassembles) the overall project scope into deliverables and supports the definition of the work effort required for effective management.
- Clearly and comprehensively defines the scope of the project in terms of deliverables that the project participants and stakeholders can understand.
- Supports documenting the accountability and responsibility for the various deliverables by having a direct relationship between the WBS elements related to the *Organizational Breakdown Structure* (OBS) identified through the *Responsibility Assignment Matrix* (RAM).

The WBS provides a structure for organizing the scope and subsequent information of the project's progress, periodic status, and projected performance for which a project manager is responsible. The WBS also supports tracking problems to their root causes to assist the project manager in identifying and implementing changes necessary to assure desired performance.

2.2.4 WBS Overview: Management

The WBS supports effective project management in several ways during the life of a project by:

- Separating the deliverable into its component parts to ensure the project plan matches the approved project scope and will fulfill the overall objectives of the project.
- Supporting the decomposition into simpler components, providing one of the primary methods for managing complex projects.
- Supporting planning and the assignment of responsibilities.
- Assisting in determining resource requirements (i.e., skills, characteristics, and so on).
- Assisting in tracking the status of resource allocations, cost estimates, expenditures, and performance.

2.2.5 WBS Overview: Organizational

The WBS provides the ability to relate the work defined to the responsible organizational units, subcontractors, or individuals. As the work and organizational responsibilities become more clearly defined, individuals (including subcontractors) are assigned responsibility for accomplishing specific WBS elements within defined budgets and schedules.

2.2.6 WBS Overview: Levels

The WBS includes all work to be done by the project stakeholders. While in some application areas the WBS consists of a three-level hierarchy describing the entire effort to be accomplished by the primary organization, that number may not be appropriate for all situations. The depth of a WBS is dependent upon the size and complexity of the project and the level of detail needed to plan and manage it.

The WBS is intended to provide a clear statement of the objectives and deliverables of the work to be performed. The WBS elements should represent identifiable work products (e.g., equipment, data, and services) encompassing the work to be performed by all parties. See appendices for examples.

2.3 SUMMARY

In summary, the WBS:

- Defines the hierarchy of deliverables
- Supports the definition of all work required to achieve an end objective or deliverable(s)
- Provides a graphical picture or textual outline of the project scope
- Provides the framework for all deliverables across the project life cycle
- Provides a vehicle for integrating and assessing schedule and cost performance
- Provides the association to the responsible stakeholders
- Facilitates the reporting and analysis of project progress and status data
- Provides a framework for specifying performance objectives.

Chapter 3

Why Use a Work Breakdown Structure?

3.1 OVERVIEW

The *PMBOK® Guide* lists the Work Breakdown Structure (WBS) as the output of project scope definition (Project Management Institute 2000). It defines project scope management as:

> The processes required to ensure that the project includes all the work required, and only the work required, to complete the project successfully (Project Management Institute 2000).

Based on this definition, the WBS has two goals:

■ To ensure that the project includes all the work needed.
■ To ensure that the project includes no unnecessary work.

Both of these goals are of great concern to the project manager. If the WBS does not meet either of these two goals, the project may fail. If necessary work is omitted, the project will almost certainly be delayed and may experience cost overruns. If unnecessary work is performed, the customer's time and money will be wasted. The WBS assists in developing a clear vision of the end product of the project and of the overall process by which it will be created, therefore, it aids in these areas.

Figure 3-5 of the *PMBOK® Guide* – 2000 Edition (reproduced in part and modified here) illustrates how the entire project plan pivots on the WBS. The WBS is the primary input to four core processes and one facilitating process:

■ Activity Definition
■ Resource Planning
■ Cost Estimating
■ Cost Budgeting
■ Risk Management Planning.

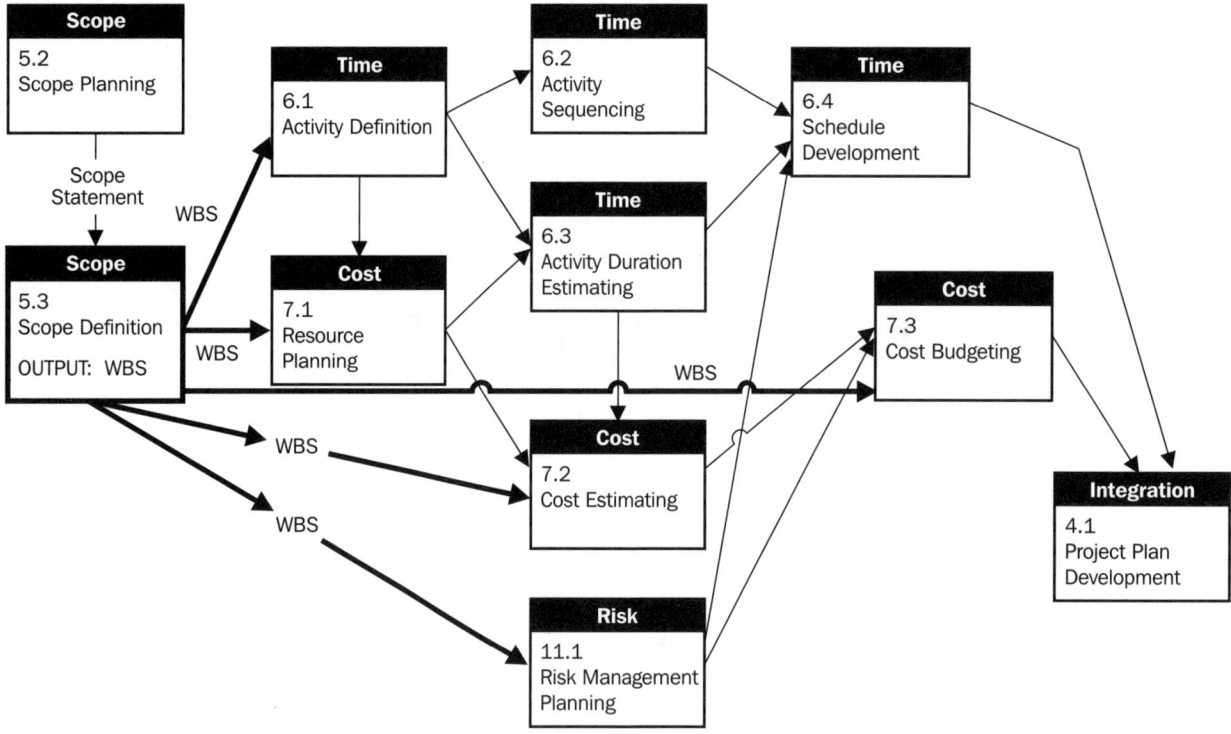

Figure 3-5 with WBS Interactions from *PMBOK® Guide* – 2000 Edition (Project Management Institute 2000)

As Figure 3-5 of the *PMBOK® Guide* illustrates, the entire project plan builds on these processes. This makes the WBS the foundation for:

■ *Coordinated and Integrated Planning*—The WBS provides the basis for integrated project management across the nine Project Management Knowledge Areas and five Project Management Process Groups. It also provides the means for using project management software to its full capability.

■ *Performance Reporting*—The WBS organizes monitoring processes, as well as the cost and schedule performance metrics associated with the work.

■ *Overall Change Control*—The WBS provides for the identification of suitable management control points that are used to facilitate communication and control scope, quality, technical soundness, schedule, and cost performance.

■ *Product Scope Management*—The WBS development process facilitates conceptualization and definition of product details.

Successful project management depends on the project manager's ability to effectively direct the project team to complete the project deliverables. Through the WBS, the work to accomplish these deliverables is structured, assigned, scheduled, tracked, and reported. Work is then directly related to the schedule and the budget, supporting effective resource allocation and tracking.

3.2 COMMUNICATIONS

The WBS facilitates communication of information regarding project scope, dependencies, risk, progress, and performance between the project manager and stakeholders throughout the life of the project. Project stakeholders include all who directly participate or have an interest in the outcome of the project, and include but are not limited to:

- Project Manager
- Project Team Members
- Customers
- Suppliers
- Management
- Regulators
- The Public/Community
- Sponsors
- Owners.

3.3 REPORTING

The WBS provides the project management team a framework on which to base project status and progress reporting. The WBS can provide different perspectives of the project structure. For example, information can be reported by:

- Life-Cycle Phase
- Deliverable
- Work Package
- All of the above compared to past similarly structured projects
- All of the above relative to cost, schedule, risk, scope, and quality perspectives.

WBS related information (like budget and schedule) can be rolled up or collapsed, to a level of detail that can be understood by the appropriate project participants and stakeholders. In addition, it can be rolled up or collapsed, to a level of detail that can be understood by the appropriate audience, such as senior or middle managers.

Chapter 4

How to Create a Work Breakdown Structure

4.1 OVERVIEW

The Work Breakdown Structure (WBS) can be created new, or it can reuse components from other WBSs. When reusing existing components, WBS elements may be drawn from previous similar projects or from standard project templates that the organization has determined support accepted best practices.

The following sections in this chapter are presented as guides for use during the development of a WBS, and contain a number of topics for consideration:

- 4.2 contains Guidelines for Preparation
- 4.3 contains Basic Assumptions or Factors
- 4.4 contains Measurement Considerations
- 4.5 includes Project Challenges for Consideration
- 4.6 aids in determining the Appropriate Level of Detail
- 4.7 discusses WBS Life-Cycle Considerations
- 4.8 addresses Risk Assessment
- 4.9 contains guidance for use when considering Resource Planning.

Some of the sections can be used as checklists for the development and refinement of the WBS.

4.2 PREPARING A WBS

The WBS evolves through an iterative consideration of the project's purpose and objectives, functional/performance design criteria, project scope, technical performance requirements, and other technical attributes. A high-level WBS can often be developed early in the conceptual stage of the project. Once the project is defined and specifications are prepared, a more detailed WBS can be developed.

The WBS can assist the project manager and stakeholders in developing a clear vision of the end product(s) of the project and of the overall process by which it will be created. With this in mind, the following should stimulate thought when developing a WBS to manage the project:

- Think through the entire project. (Look at dividing high-level deliverables.)
- Think deliverables. (What is to be provided/what is required?)
- Think with the end in mind. (How will this component contribute to the finished deliverable?)
- Think through the production of the deliverables. (What methods? What special processes? What quality requirements? What inspections?)

Have you formulated a vision of the final product in your mind?

- What are its constituent parts?
- How do the pieces work together?
- What needs to be done?

These thoughts and questions are intended to help the project manager develop a clear statement of what the product of the project is—and to help answer the question, "How does one eat an elephant?" Answer: "One bite at a time!" The WBS is the technique for dividing "the elephant" into bite-sized pieces.

The following steps describe the general process for developing a WBS:

- Step 1: Identify the final product(s) of the project—what must be delivered to achieve project success. A thorough review of high-level project scope documents (inputs such as *statement of work* [SOW], technical requirements documents, and so on) is recommended to ensure consistency between the WBS and the project requirements.
- Step 2: Define the product's major deliverables, which are often predecessor deliverables necessary for the project, but that in themselves do not satisfy a business need (e.g., a design specification).
- Step 3: Decompose major deliverables to a level of detail appropriate for management and integrated control. These WBS elements normally tie to clear and discrete identification of stand-alone deliverable products.
- Step 4: Review and refine the WBS until project stakeholders agree that project planning can be successfully completed and that execution and control will successfully produce the desired outcomes.

4.3 FACTORS TO BE CONSIDERED

In developing a WBS, the following basic assumptions should be considered:

- Each WBS element should represent a single tangible deliverable.
- Each WBS element should represent an aggregation of all subordinate WBS elements listed immediately below it.
- Each subordinate WBS element must belong to only one single parent (or superior) WBS element.
- The deliverables should be logically decomposed to the level that represents how they will be produced (designed, purchased, subcontracted, fabricated). The partitioning of deliverables from higher levels within the WBS to lower levels must be logically related.

- Deliverables must be unique and distinct from their peers, and should be decomposed to the level of detail needed to plan and manage the work to obtain or create them.
- Deliverables should be clearly defined to eliminate duplication of effort within WBS elements, across organizations, or between individuals responsible for completing the work.
- Deliverables should be limited in size and definition for effective control—but not so small as to make cost of control excessive and not so large as to make the item unmanageable or the risk unacceptable.
- The WBS development process should provide a vehicle for flexibility, particularly when the scope of the project effort may change. A well-managed project, however, will incorporate a rigorous change control process to document and manage *scope changes*. When work scope changes do take place, the WBS must be updated.
- Each entry in the WBS representing subcontracted or externally committed deliverables should directly correspond to matching entries in the subcontractor's WBS.
- All deliverables are explicitly included in the WBS.
- All significant reporting items (e.g., review meetings, monthly reports, test reports, and so on) are included and identified in the WBS.
- All WBS elements should be compatible with organizational and accounting structures.
- A coding scheme for WBS elements that clearly represents the hierarchical structure when viewed in text format should be used.
- Technical input should be obtained from knowledgeable technical subject matter experts (SMEs), and communicated to and validated by other key SMEs assigned to the project.

4.4 WBS MEASUREMENT CONSIDERATIONS

It is strongly recommended that project management activities foster measurement of work accomplishment, as opposed to goal achievement by providing an integrated view across project components. Proper linking between the WBS and associated cost and schedule is critical if integrated analysis of cost, schedule, and performance is to be accomplished. In doing so, the project manager should keep the following in mind:

- Cost and schedule impacts can be determined only if there is a clear link between performance parameters and budgeted work packages via the WBS. This link is accomplished in order to obtain a "performance budget baseline" or the budget associated at the work package level.
- All work in the WBS must be estimated, resourced, scheduled, budgeted, and controlled. The WBS has two parts: the structure and the component definition. It is the mechanism that divides and organizes the work scope into units of work so that each unit can be estimated, resourced, scheduled, budgeted, and controlled while progress is reported.
- Where there is a clear link between performance parameters and budgeted work packages via the WBS, the linkage should be made at a high level within the WBS. All work packages can then be associated with the performance parameters.

■ Separate WBS elements should be included for integration *tasks* where several components are being brought together to create a higher-level WBS element. By identifying the integration work separately where ever the above occurs, performance measurement information will provide a timely indication that problems are emerging. Cost and schedule variances occurring in WBS elements that contain integration work can also indicate potential future rework in areas that have previously been completed. When these trends are projected, the result could be a far greater impact on revised estimates at completion than from projections of trends in other areas. Technical experts can provide guidance regarding potential integration problems, which can help the project manager decide whether or not to create these separate integration and assembly (I&A) WBS elements.

■ Identification and tracking of performance metrics in a disciplined and systematic fashion helps provide significant early warning of potential problems and their nature.

4.5 CHALLENGES TO BE CONSIDERED

Challenges associated with developing the WBS include:

■ Balancing the project definition aspects of the WBS with the data collecting and reporting requirements. (Remember that the primary purpose of the WBS is to define the project's scope through the decomposition of deliverables.) Each WBS is a tool designed to assist the project manager with decomposition of the project only to the levels necessary to meet the needs of the project, the nature of the work, and the confidence of the team. Excessive WBS levels may require unrealistic levels of maintenance and reporting.

■ Developing a WBS that defines the logical relationships among all the components of the project. This is generally clarified through the use of a dependency network in the project schedule.

■ Ensuring the development and utilization of the WBS. Omitting WBS development and proceeding directly to the network diagram (such as a Gantt chart, CPM Schedule, or Precedence Diagram) may lead to unforeseen and unexpected difficulty, including project delay.

■ Avoiding the creation of WBS elements that are not deliverable-focused (for example, structuring the WBS strictly by process or organization). WBS elements that are not deliverable-focused may lead to project failure.

■ Defining WBS elements representing opening and closing stages such as planning, assembly, and testing.

■ Identifying and detailing all key project deliverables (e.g., regulatory permits, packaging, distribution, or marketing).

■ Preventing the use of WBS elements that define overlapping responsibilities for the creation of a deliverable(s). Each WBS element must have one person who is clearly accountable for its completion.

■ Identifying key project management work such as:
   ■ process management
   ■ services and provisioning
   ■ information/communication
   ■ administrative documentation, training, and software.

These should be defined as level-of-effort WBS elements in those cases where they may be interim deliverables, do not themselves generate discrete deliverables, and may not be included in the final project deliverables.

4.6 WBS LEVEL OF DETAIL

4.6.1 Overview

The WBS development process has been described as proceeding to successive levels of increasing detail until a level is reached that provides the needed insight for effective project management. This process can be summarized in the checklist in Section 4.6.2, which provides guidance for determining the need for further decomposition of the work. If the answers to most of the items in the checklist are positive, then further decomposition should be considered. The greater the number of positive answers to the questions in Section 4.6.2, the stronger the justification for further division of some or all of the WBS.

Note: Not all legs of the WBS must be symmetrical in terms of the number of levels developed. There is no need to decompose all legs of the WBS if the need is only present in one area.

4.6.2 Determining Appropriate WBS Level of Detail

Should the WBS be decomposed further? Questions for consideration:

- Is there a need to improve the accuracy of the cost and duration estimates of the WBS element?
- Is more than one individual or group responsible for the WBS element? While there may be a variety of resources assigned to a WBS element, there should be one individual assigned overall responsibility for the deliverable created during the completion of the WBS element.
- Does the WBS element content include more than one type of work process or more than one deliverable?
- Is there a need to precisely know the timing of work processes internal to the WBS element?
- Is there a need to separately define the cost of work processes or deliverables internal to the WBS element?
- Are there dependencies between deliverables within a WBS element to another WBS element?
- Are there significant time gaps in the execution of the work processes internal to the WBS element?
- Do resource requirements change over time within a WBS element?
- Do prerequisites differ among internal deliverables within the WBS element?
- Are clear, objective criteria missing for measuring progress for the WBS element?
- Are there acceptance criteria applicable before the completion of the entire WBS element?
- Are there specific risks that require focused attention to a portion of the WBS element?
- Can a portion of the work to be performed within the WBS element be scheduled as a unit?

- Is the WBS element clearly and completely understood to the satisfaction of the project manager, project team members, and other stakeholders—including the customer?
- Is there a stakeholder interested in analyzing status and performance of only a portion of the work covered by the WBS element?

As identified earlier, the level of the detail in a WBS is a function of the size of the project and a balance between complexity, risk, and the project manager's need for control. The level of detail may also vary during the evolution of a project. A top-down and bottom-up analysis of the WBS can clarify whether the WBS is both complete and defined at the proper level of detail.

Short-duration projects may lend themselves to decomposition to appropriate levels of detail at the outset, while projects of longer duration and higher complexity may preclude decomposition of all deliverables until further in the future. Again, this may mean that on any given project, some portions of the WBS may have different levels of decomposition. This is especially true when doing *rolling wave planning*, where the plan is detailed for the immediately upcoming work only and work far in the future is defined at a high level until later in the project life cycle.

4.7 WBS LIFE-CYCLE CONSIDERATIONS

Decomposition of complex requirements into simpler components provides one of the primary methods for handling complex projects. WBS development is the technique for accomplishing this decomposition. In structuring the WBS, one must look to the future and determine how the work will be accomplished and managed. The WBS should reflect this structure. In addition to strict end-product identification, the WBS may also reflect level-of-effort functions such as project management activities and life-cycle timing (*project phases*). These other elements should only be used, however, to the required level of detail necessary to organize the work tasks. Remember that each of the lowest-level WBS elements should reflect work with specific, tangible deliverables.

4.8 PROJECT RISK AND THE WBS

4.8.1 Overview

For projects with highly related risk factors, a more detailed WBS is strongly suggested. The *risk events*—events that might have a detrimental impact on the project—are evaluated to identify and characterize specific risks.

Project risk is related to the likelihood of events positively or adversely affecting project objectives, including key elements such as technical design, quality, cost, and schedule. The WBS decomposition approach may assist in risk identification and mitigation. For instance, projects that require permits and approvals from regulatory authorities can be high risk. Since risk can impact several WBS elements, it would be prudent for the project manager to perform impact analyses against all WBS elements, thus isolating the risks, providing for individual treatment, and permitting more effective focus for risk management.

©2001 Project Management Institute, Four Campus Boulevard, Newtown Square, PA 19073-3299 USA

The first step in this technique is to review the WBS elements to the level being considered and segment them into risk events. This review should consider the critical areas (requirements analysis/development, design and engineering, technology, logistics, and so on) and other factors that may help to describe risk events. Using information from a variety of sources such as program plans, prior risk assessments, and expert interviews, the risk events are examined within critical areas to determine the probability of occurrence, severity of consequence (impact), and interdependency.

The risks associated with an effort may also define the level of detail necessary. Additional detail in high-risk areas provides for better assumption definition, as well as improved cost estimates and time assessment. This forced structuring provides an opportunity to define the assumptions and expectations at a controllable level.

Risk planning can be incorporated directly into the WBS by defining and including contingency activities as successors to the risk-impacted activities. The duration of the contingency activities are set to compensate for the degree of uncertainty and potential impact of the risk event. As an example, a permit-contingency activity could be created as a successor to the permit-application activity. The duration of the permit-application activity is set to the normal time period expected for a permit application, and the duration of the contingency activity is set to reflect the probability and impact of the risk of delay.

4.8.2 The Relationship between Project Risk and the WBS

The following questions should be addressed for each WBS element when considering project risk:

- Are the deliverables completely and clearly defined?
- Will the quality of the work be evaluated through efforts such as testing and inspection?
- What is the likelihood of change?
- Is the technology changing faster than the project can be accomplished?
- Have manpower, facilities capability, availability of internal resources, and potential suppliers been checked?
- Is extensive subcontracting expected?
- Is management committed to the project and will they provide the support needed?
- Are requirements defined and approved?
- Has a formal change process been defined and implemented?
- Have metrics been defined for how the deliverables will be measured?
- Have resource requirements been identified for development of the project deliverables?
- Have other risks been identified, including stakeholder buy-in, public relations, management approval, team understanding, and project opposition?
- Has a communication plan (internal and external) been defined and implemented?
- Are third-party dependencies understood and monitored for change?
- Have alternate suppliers of required products, supplies, or expertise been identified?

4.9 RESOURCE PLANNING, MANAGEMENT, AND THE WBS

4.9.1 Overview

The WBS is decomposed to the level necessary to plan and manage the work. Normally this will be at least one level below the reporting requirements—one that allows for the effective planning, control, and performance measurement of discrete activities with uniquely identifiable resources.

Although full resource identification will come later in the planning process, it can be useful to understand in general how that will be done, and ensure that the level of detail in the WBS will support those efforts.

4.9.2 Resource Planning and Management

In order to prepare for adequate resource planning against the WBS, consider the following when examining the WBS level of detail:

- Is all the work planned to a degree of detail necessary to make and keep commitments?
- Is there an ability to establish and manage individual work assignments with the reporting structure indicated by this WBS?
- Can work assignments be established from a progressive expansion of the WBS?
- How will work generally be assigned and controlled?
- Will it be possible to reconcile individual work assignments to the formal scheduling system?
- How will budgets be established?
- Will it be possible to relate the budget to the proposed work assignments?
- Is the level of detail in the WBS appropriate for effective planning and control?
- Is the work defined by the WBS grouped in a logical manner?
- Is more than one organization involved (indicating the need to validate the WBS with others before doing detailed resource planning)?
- How will the status of work in progress be determined?

4.10 ADDITIONAL CONSIDERATIONS

The interrelationships between the specification of requirements, the WBS, the statement of work, resource plans, and the master and detailed schedules provides specific information relative to the relationship among cost, schedule, and performance.

Once the WBS is developed, it is important that the project manager and other stakeholders involved in the management of the project know "how things are going" on a regular basis. In this regard:

- Think reporting and control mechanisms.
- How will WBS element completion be determined?

Appendix A

The Project Management Institute Standards-Setting Process

The Project Management Institute (PMI) Standards-Setting Process was established initially as Institute policy by a vote of the PMI Board of Directors at its October 1993 meeting. In March 1998, the PMI Board of Directors approved modifications to the process. Then in March 1999, it was modified again to make it consistent with the concurrent change in PMI governance procedures, approved by the PMI Executive Director, and provided to the PMI Board of Directors.

A.1 PMI STANDARDS DOCUMENTS

PMI Standards Documents are those developed or published by PMI that describe generally accepted practices of project management, specifically:
- *A Guide to the Project Management Body of Knowledge* (*PMBOK® Guide*)
- *PMI Practice Standard for Work Breakdown Structures*
- Project Management Body of Knowledge Handbooks.

Additional documents may be added to this list by the PMI Standards Manager, subject to the advice and consent of the PMI Project Management Standards Program Member Advisory Group and the PMI Executive Director. Standards Documents may be original works published by PMI, or they may be publications of other organizations or individuals.

Standards Documents will be developed in accordance with the Code of Good Practice for Standardization developed by the International Organization for Standardization (ISO) and the standards development guidelines established by the American National Standards Institute.

A.2 DEVELOPMENT OF ORIGINAL WORKS

Standards Documents that are original works developed by PMI, or revisions of such documents, will be handled as follows:

- Prospective developer(s) will submit a proposal to the PMI Standards Manager. The Manager may also request such proposals. The Manager will submit all received proposals to the PMI Standards Program Member Advisory Group who, with the Manager, will decide whether to accept or reject each proposal.
- The Manager will inform the prospective developer(s) as to the decision and the rationale for the decision. If an approved proposal requires funding in excess of that budgeted for standards development, the Manager will submit the proposal to the PMI Executive Director for funding.
- For all approved and funded proposals, the Manager will support the developer's efforts so as to maximize the probability that the end product will be accepted. Developer(s) will be required to sign the PMI Volunteer Assignment of Copyright.
- When the proposed material has been completed to the satisfaction of the developer(s), the developer(s) will submit the material to the PMI Standards Manager. The PMI Standards Program Member Advisory Group, with the Manager, will review the proposed material and decide whether to initiate further review by knowledgeable individuals or request additional work by the developer(s).
- The Manager will appoint, subject to review and approval by the PMI Standards Program Member Advisory Group, at least three knowledgeable individuals to review and comment on the material. Based on comments received, the Member Advisory Group will decide whether to accept the material as an Exposure Draft.
- The PMI Standards Manager will develop a plan for obtaining appropriate public review for each Exposure Draft. The plan will include a) a review period of not less than one month and not more than six months, b) announcement of the availability of the Exposure Draft for review in the *PM Network* (and/or any other similarly appropriate publication media), and c) cost of review copies. The PMI Standards Program Member Advisory Group must approve the Manager's plan for public review. Each Exposure Draft will include a notice asking for comments to be sent to the PMI Standards Manager at PMI Headquarters and noting the length of and expiration date for the review period.
- Exposure Drafts will be published under the aegis of the PMI Publishing Department and must meet the standards of that group regarding typography and style.
- During the review period, the Manager will solicit the formal input of the Managers of other PMI Programs (e.g., Certification, Education, Components, and Publishing) that may be affected by the future publication of the material as a PMI Standard.
- At the conclusion of the review period, the PMI Standards Manager will review comments received with the PMI Standards Program Member Advisory Group and will work with the developer(s) and others as needed to incorporate appropriate comments. If the comments are major, the PMI Standards Program Member Advisory Group may elect to repeat the Exposure Draft review process.
- When the PMI Standards Manager and the PMI Standards Program Member Advisory Group have approved a proposed PMI Standards Document, the Manager will promptly submit the document to the PMI Executive Director for final review and approval. The PMI Executive Director will verify compliance with procedures and ensure that member input was sufficient. The PMI Executive

Director will a) approve the document as submitted; b) reject the document; or c) request additional review, and will provide explanatory comments in support of the chosen option.

A.3 ADOPTION OF NON-ORIGINAL WORKS AS STANDARDS

Standards Documents that are the work of other organizations or individuals will be handled as follows:

- Any person or organization may submit a request to the PMI Standards Manager to consider a non-PMI publication as a PMI Standard. The Manager will submit all proposals received to the PMI Standards Program Member Advisory Group who, with the Manager, will decide whether to accept or reject each proposal. If accepted, the Manager will appoint, subject to review and approval by the PMI Standards Program Member Advisory Group, at least three knowledgeable individuals to review and comment on the material.

- During the review period, the Manager will solicit the formal input of the Managers of other PMI Programs (e.g., Certification, Education, Components, and Publishing) that may be affected by the future publication of the material as a PMI Standard.

- Based on comments received, the Member Advisory Group, with the Manager, will decide whether to a) accept the proposal as written as a PMI Standard, b) accept the proposal with modifications and/or an addendum as a PMI Standard, c) seek further review and comment on the proposal (that is, additional reviewers and/or issuance as an Exposure Draft), or d) reject the proposal. The Manager will inform the submitter as to the decision and the rationale for the decision.

- When the PMI Standards Manager and the PMI Standards Program Member Advisory Group have approved a proposed PMI Standards Document, the Manager will promptly submit the document to the PMI Executive Director for final review and approval. The Manager will prepare a proposal for the PMI Executive Director for consideration of a prospective relationship with the owner(s) of the material.

- The PMI Executive Director will verify compliance with procedures and will ensure that member input was sufficient. The PMI Executive Director will a) approve the document as submitted; b) reject the document; or c) request additional review, and will provide explanatory comments in support of the chosen option.

Appendix B

Evolution of the Project Management Institute Practice Standard for Work Breakdown Structures

During the development and subsequent publication by the Project Management Institute (PMI®) of *A Guide to the Project Management Body of Knowledge (PMBOK® Guide)*, it was recognized that project management practitioners and other stakeholders would be aided by more in-depth treatment of the listed inputs, tools and techniques, and outputs. Consequently, in early 1998, PMI asked for volunteers to develop the first such practice standard, specifically on the Work Breakdown Structure (WBS). A volunteer team was assembled and during the year worked through a number of drafts and revision cycles.

In early 1999, the PMI Project Management Standards Program Team reviewed the draft and recommended the completion of the *Practice Standard*. In late spring 1999, Kim Colenso was approved as the new project manager for the *Practice Standard*. He was tasked to form a new team to make minor modifications to the current draft, and add example WBSs. The plan was to publish the *Project Management Institute Practice Standard for Work Breakdown Structures* in an Exposure Draft to the PMI membership and other affected parties by the summer of 2000, and a final document would be published as a PMI Standard in 2001.

A team was assembled during the summer and fall of 1999 through solicitation of participation from the PMI Specific Interest Groups and other volunteer sources. During this period, a controversy developed within the project team on whether or not an *activity* was or should be part of the WBS. Through further discussion among the project team and among the PMI Project Management Standards Program Member Advisory Group, the issue was resolved, and an article describing the outcome was published in *PM Network* in April 2000 (see References).

The project team implemented a formal change-control procedure to guide and control the evolution of the *Practice Standard*. This procedure required all proposed changes to be documented and approved by the project team. As a result of this process, the following events occurred:

- Over forty formal change requests were submitted and approved by the team between October 1999 and April 2000. Another six were disapproved, as the arguments were deemed unpersuasive.
- Eleven WBS examples were approved and incorporated as Appendices E through O of this *Practice Standard*.

The revised draft was submitted to the PMI Project Management Standards Program Team in May 2000 for consideration as the Exposure Draft to be circulated among PMI membership and other affected parties. Following approval by the PMI Project Management Standards Program Team, the proposed Exposure Draft was submitted for formal review to six other knowledge experts. The team evaluated the comments from these six reviewers and the PMI Project Management Standards Program Team. A final draft was then submitted to the PMI Project Management Standards Program Team and approved for the Exposure Draft.

The Exposure Draft was submitted for public review on 29 September 2000, with an exposure closure on 30 November 2000. During this period, 488 comments were received. Due to the constraints of the review process, each idea proposed during the review was evaluated against the potential for delaying the schedule to incorporate new material and the subsequent impact to information that had been previously established in the draft. As in all successful projects, there is a tradeoff between quality, cost, and schedule. In this case all comments that the project team accepted for the current version have been incorporated.

When we look at the current *PMBOK® Guide – 2000 Edition*, it is a remarkable achievement. It has gone through an evolutionary process for fourteen years. Each edition has improved upon the previous version. After several editions, the result is an extremely refined and powerful document. The same will be true for the *Project Management Institute Practice Standard for Work Breakdown Structures*. It has gone through its initial development. Now it is ready to begin its journey through the refinement process.

Appendix C

Contributors and Reviewers

1998 PROJECT TEAM

Contributors

- George Belev, Knolls Atomic Power Laboratory, WBS Practice Standard Project Manager
- Ed Kilner, PMP, Project Solutions Unlimited
- Kim Colenso, PMP, Blue Cross Blue Shield of Colorado

1999/2001 PROJECT TEAM

Contributors

- Kim Colenso, PMP, Artemis Management Systems, WBS Practice Standard Project Manager
- Ron Stein, ARCADIS, Environmental Management WBS Example Team Leader, Exposure Review Core Team
- Nigel B. Blampied, PMP, California Department of Transportation, Exposure Review Core Team
- Wayne Stottler, Kepner-Tregoe
- Ben Voivedich
- Ed Smith, Qwest-Apptimum, Exposure Review Core Team
- Eric S. Norman, Getronics Inc., Exposure Review Core Team
- Carl Wetzel, Shell Services International, Inc, Exposure Review Core Team
- Darrel G. Hubbard, MACTEC, Inc., Exposure Review Core Team
- Robert Youker, World Bank, Retired
- Mikkel Hansen, Texaco Upstream Technology, OGP WBS Example Team Leader
- Nathan Lewis, Eli Lilly and Company, Pharmaceutical WBS Example Team Leader
- Dr. Jann Nielsen, Eli Lilly and Company (contributed to WBS example)
- Dr. Jim McDonough, Eli Lilly and Company (contributed to WBS example)

Reviewers

- Allan Mikoff, Project Management Resources, WBS Example Review Team Leader
- Kim-Mei Lim, Unisys Msc Sdn Bhd
- John Schlicter, The Weather Channel
- Jim Peters, SoftwareMatters.com, Inc.
- Rick Trites, Human Resources Development Canada
- Wesley Sturgis
- Janet Murray, USAA Federal Savings Bank
- Stephen Mattera, Nokia
- Margery J. Cruise, Cruise 8 Associates
- Monica Rousset, American General Life
- John Waterbury, Fleet Bank
- James W. Parcels, Commonwealth of Pennsylvania
- E. N. Friesen, Seagull Consulting
- Linda Salac, State of Nebraska Health & Human Services
- Wayne Abba
- Neil F. Albert, GRC International, MCR Federal, Inc.

PMI '99 STANDARDS SESSION VOLUNTEERS

The following individuals worked in a team setting during the Project Management Institute '99 Standards Program Open Working Session to create example Work Breakdown Structures. These were used as delivered by the team members or as the basis for several of the examples that appear in this document.

- Robert Trafton, Merant
- Eric S. Norman, Getronics Inc.
- Connie Inman, Encore Development
- Dean A. Hoffer, Fermi National Accelerator Laboratory
- Scott Freauf, PMSI–Project Mentors
- Warren Nogaki, JPL/Caltech
- Margery J. Cruise, SPMgroup Ltd.
- Darrell Hubbard, MACTEC, Inc.
- James W. Parcels, Commonwealth of Pennsylvania
- Dr. Al Zeitoun, International Institute for Learning, Inc.
- Craig Garvin, IT Corporation
- Ed Smith, Sun Microsystems, Inc.
- Bradford Nelson, Lockheed Martin Federal Systems

PMI STANDARDS PROGRAM MEMBER ADVISORY GROUP 1999–2001

- George Belev, KAPL, Inc.–A Lockheed Martin Company
- Cynthia A. Berg, PMP, Medtronic Microelectronics Center
- Sergio R. Coronado, ExperienceApplication.com
- J. Brian Hobbs, PMP, University of Quebec at Montreal
- Tom Kurihara, TKstds Management
- Bobbye Underwood, PMP, Concert

SELECTED REVIEWERS OF PRE-EXPOSURE DRAFT

These volunteers provided specific evaluations and comments on the pre-exposure draft. The project team and the PMI Standards Program Team considered their input in the development of the Exposure Draft.

- William Bahnmaier, US DoD Defense Systems Management College
- Don Campbell, Horne Engineering Services
- Scott Campbell, PMP, DMR Consulting
- Fred Manzer, PMP, Welkin Associates
- Regina Santarcangelo, PMP, SoftKey, Inc.
- Max Smith, Compaq Computer Corporation

SELECTED REVIEWERS OF EXPOSURE DRAFT

The following individuals provided comments and/or recommendations on the exposure draft of this docuemnt and reviewed this document.

- Jean-Jacques Aureglia, PMP
- Nigel B. Blampied, PMP
- Walter O. Bowman, PMP
- J. Chris Boyd
- Dennis H. Carignan
- Frank Carney
- Gene D. Carlow, PMP
- Kim C. Caruthers, PMP
- Bruce C. Chadbourne, PMP
- Michael T. Clark, PMP
- Elizabeth Clarke
- John E. Cormier, PMP
- James C. Davis, PMP
- Quentin W. Fleming
- Pablo P. Flores V, PMP
- Roy C. Greenia, PMP
- Roger K. Goodman
- Fumio Hamano, PMP
- Christopher Herbert, PMP
- Lewis D. Kana, PMP
- Suen Kuo-Tsai
- Blase T. Kwok, PMP
- Craig Letavec
- Susan Long
- Warren Marquis
- Adan Lopez Miranda, PMP
- Peter McCarthy
- Robert McCormack, PMP
- Randy T. McIntyre, PMP
- Gordon R. Miller
- Bert Mosterd, PMP
- Rita Mulcahy, PMP
- Jeffrey S. Nielsen, PMP
- John O'Neill

- Kasuhiko Okubo, PE, PMP
- James E. O'Quinn, PMP
- Jerry L. Partridge, PMP
- Carol Personick, PMP
- Taras Pich
- Patrick Pichon
- Kenneth Robson, PMP
- George G. Seidler, PMP
- Jean M. Sekula, PMP
- Karen M. Senn, PMP
- Shoukat M. Sheikh, MBA, PMP
- Kazuo Shimizu, PMP
- Larry Sieck
- W. G. Simpson
- Nancy L. Singletary, PMP
- Greg J. Skulmoski
- Joyce A. Statz, PMP
- Russell B. Sturm, PMP
- George Sukumar, PE
- Mark W. Swarthout Esq.
- Judy L. Van Meter
- Franco Vervloet, PMP
- William W. Wassel, PMP
- K. Watkins, PMP
- S. J. Westermann
- Tammo T. Wilkens, PE, PMP
- Eddie R. Williams, PMP
- Thomas Williamson, PMP
- Rick Woods, MBA, PMP, CCP

PMI HEADQUARTERS STAFF

- Steven L. Fahrenkrog, PMP, PMI Standards Manager
- Iesha Brown, PMI Standards Associate
- Lew Gedansky, PMI Research Manager
- Eva Goldman, PMI Technical Research & Standards Associate

PMI PUBLISHING DIVISION STAFF

- Linda Cherry, PMI Publisher
- Dewey Messer, PMI Special Projects Administrator
- Toni Knott, PMI Editor, Book Division
- Michelle Owen, PMI Graphic Designer
- Lisa Fisher, PMI Publishing Coordinator
- Galadriel La Vere, PMI Freelance Editor

Appendix D

Guidelines for a Project Management Institute Practice Standard

- Each practice standard provides guidelines on the mechanics (e.g., nuts and bolts, basics, fundamentals, step-by-step usage guide, how it operates, how to do it) of some significant process (input, tool, technique, or output) that is relevant to a project manager.
- A practice standard does not necessarily mirror the life-cycle phases of many projects. But, an individual practice standard may be applicable to the completion of one or more phases within a project.
- A practice standard does not necessarily mirror the knowledge areas within *A Guide to the Project Management Body of Knowledge (PMBOK® Guide)*, although an individual practice standard will provide sufficient detail and background for one or more of the inputs, tools and techniques, and/or outputs. Therefore, practice standards are not required to use the name of any knowledge area.
- Each practice standard should include information on *what* the significant process is and does, *why* it is significant, *how* to perform it, *when* it should be performed and, if necessary for further clarification, *who* should perform it.
- Each practice standard should include information that is accepted and applicable for most projects most of the time within the project management community. Processes that are generally restricted or applicable to one industry, country, or companion profession (i.e., an application area) may be included as an appendix for informational purpose, rather than part of the practice standard. With strong support and evidence, an application area-specific process may be considered as an *extension* practice standard, in the same manner as extensions to the *PMBOK® Guide* are considered.
- Each practice standard will benefit from the inclusion of examples and templates. It is best when an example or template includes a discussion of its strengths and weaknesses. A background description may be necessary to put this discussion in the appropriate context. The examples should be aligned with the relevant information in the standard or its appendix and placed in proximity to that information.

- All practice standards will be written in the same general style and format.
- Each practice standard project will assess the need to align with or reference other practice standards.
- Each practice standard will be consistent with the *PMBOK® Guide*.
- Each practice standard is intended to be more prescriptive than the *PMBOK® Guide*.

Appendix E

Oil, Gas, and Petrochemical (OGP) WBS Example

PRODUCTION PLATFORM PROJECT WBS

This is an example of a WBS, from the owner's point of view, for the detailed design, fabrication, and installation of an offshore production platform. As the detailed engineering, fabrication, and installation are distinct phases of the work, these are placed at level 1 of the WBS. This fits with the progression of the work, but also with the contracting strategy; i.e. different contractors for engineering, for fabrication, and so on may be employed or used.

1.0 Project Management

1.1 Project Management
- 1.1.1 Project Direction and Procedures
- 1.1.2 Project Planning & Scheduling and Cost
- 1.1.3 Progress Reports, Monthly Reports, etc.

1.2 Project Control
- 1.2.1 Document Control
- 1.2.2 Interface Control

2.0 Detailed Engineering

2.1 General
- 2.1.1 Audit by and Contractor's Acceptance of Preliminary Engineering
- 2.1.2 Design Basis and Specifications
- 2.1.3 Calculations and Engineering Data Books
- 2.1.4 Summary Reports
- 2.1.5 Platform Equipment Manuals

2.2 *Jacket*

- 2.2.1 Structural Engineering & Drafting
  - 2.2.1.1 Jacket In-Service Analyses
  - 2.2.1.2 Jacket Pre-Service Analyses
  - 2.2.1.3 Jacket Design Details
  - 2.2.1.4 Jacket Cathodic Protection
  - 2.2.1.5 Jacket Weights and Material Takeoffs
  - 2.2.1.6 Jacket Approved for Construction (AFC) Drawings
  - 2.2.1.7 Jacket Detailed Engineering and Design Report
- 2.2.2 Mechanical Engineering & Drafting
  - 2.2.2.1 Flood & Vent System
  - 2.2.2.2 Grouting System

2.3 *Piling*

- 2.3.1 Structural Engineering & Drafting
  - 2.3.1.1 Piling In-Service Analyses
  - 2.3.1.2 Piling Pre-Service Analyses
  - 2.3.1.3 Piling Design Details
  - 2.3.1.4 Piling Weights and Material Takeoffs
  - 2.3.1.5 Piling AFC Drawings
  - 2.3.1.6 Piling Detailed Engineering and Design Report

2.4 *Topsides*

- 2.4.1 Structural Engineering & Drafting
  - 2.4.1.1 Deck In-Service Analyses
  - 2.4.1.2 Deck Pre-Service Analyses
  - 2.4.1.3 Deck Design Details
  - 2.4.1.4 Deck Weights and Material Takeoffs
  - 2.4.1.5 Deck AFC Drawings
  - 2.4.1.6 Deck Detailed Engineering and Design Report
- 2.4.2 Mechanical/Process Engineering & Drafting
  - 2.4.2.1 Process Simulation/Calculations
  - 2.4.2.2 Equipment Design/Sizing
  - 2.4.2.3 Pipe Stress Analysis
  - 2.4.2.4 Hazard Analysis
  - 2.4.2.5 Specifications, Data Sheets, and Request for Quotations
  - 2.4.2.6 Vendor Data Reviews
  - 2.4.2.7 Weight, Material Takeoffs, Bill of Materials
  - 2.4.2.8 AFC Drawings for:
    - 2.4.2.8.1 Process Flow Diagrams/Utility Flow Diagrams
    - 2.4.2.8.2 Mechanical Flow Diagrams/Piping & Instrument Drawings
    - 2.4.2.8.3 Equipment Layouts/Arrangements/Skid Layouts
    - 2.4.2.8.4 Piping Supports
    - 2.4.2.8.5 Piping General Arrangements, Elevations, and Isometrics
    - 2.4.2.8.6 Other AFC Drawings
  - 2.4.2.9 Data Books, Equipment Manuals, Engineering and Design Report

2.4.3   Electrical Engineering & Drafting
- 2.4.3.1   Electrical Engineering and Design
- 2.4.3.2   Electrical Specifications, Data Sheets, and Request for Quotations
- 2.4.3.3   Electrical Load Study/List
- 2.4.3.4   Vendor Data Reviews
- 2.4.3.5   Weight, Material Takeoffs, Bill of Materials
- 2.4.3.6   AFC Drawings for:
  - 2.4.3.6.1   Area Classifications
  - 2.4.3.6.2   Electrical Symbol Legend
  - 2.4.3.6.3   Electrical One-Line Drawings
  - 2.4.3.6.4   Schematics/Schedule/Plans
  - 2.4.3.6.5   Buildings and Equipment Layouts
  - 2.4.3.6.6   Electrical Arrangement and Cable Tray Routing
  - 2.4.3.6.7   Electrical Installation Details
  - 2.4.3.6.8   Other AFC Drawings
- 2.4.3.7   Data Books, Equipment Manuals, Engineering and Design Report

2.4.4   Instrument Engineering & Drafting
- 2.4.4.1   Instrument Engineering & Design
- 2.4.4.2   Fire & Safety Engineering & Design
- 2.4.4.3   Relief Systems Sizing Calculations
- 2.4.4.4   Instrument Specification, Data Sheets, and Request for Quotations
- 2.4.4.5   Instrument Index
- 2.4.4.6   Vendor Data Reviews

2.4.5   Weight, Material Takeoffs, Bill of Materials

2.4.6   AFC Drawings for:
- 2.4.6.1   SAFE Charts/PSFDs
- 2.4.6.2   Control Panels
- 2.4.6.3   PLC System
- 2.4.6.4   Tubing Tray Routing
- 2.4.6.5   Loop Diagrams
- 2.4.6.6   Instrument Installation Details
- 2.4.6.7   Fire & Safety
- 2.4.6.8   Pressure Relief Systems
- 2.4.6.9   Other AFC Drawings

2.4.7   Data Books, Equipment Manuals, Engineering and Design Reports

3.0 Procurement

3.1 General

3.1.1   Procurement Procedures

3.1.2   Expediting & Inspection Procedures

3.2 *Jacket*
- 3.2.1 Owner Furnished Equipment (OFE)
- 3.2.2 Contractor Furnished Reimbursable Equipment (CFRE)
- 3.2.3 All Other Contractor Supplied Equipment
- 3.2.4 Bulk Materials—Contractor Supplied
  - 3.2.4.1 Structural
  - 3.2.4.2 Anodes

3.3 *Piling*
- 3.3.1 Bulk Materials—Contractor Supplied
  - 3.3.1.1 Structural
  - 3.3.1.2 etc.

3.4 *Topsides*
- 3.4.1 Owner Furnished Equipment (OFE)
  - 3.4.1.1 Rotating Equipment
  - 3.4.1.2 Pressure Vessels
  - 3.4.1.3 Electrical Generation
  - 3.4.1.4 etc.
- 3.4.2 Contractor Furnished Reimbursable Equipment (CFRE)
  - 3.4.2.1 Rotating Equipment
  - 3.4.2.2 Pressure Vessels
  - 3.4.2.3 Other CFRE
- 3.4.3 All Other Contractor Supplied Equipment
- 3.4.4 Bulk Materials—Contractor Supplied
  - 3.4.4.1 Structural
  - 3.4.4.2 Piping, Valves, & Fittings
  - 3.4.4.3 Electrical
  - 3.4.4.4 Instrument
  - 3.4.4.5 etc.

4.0 Fabrication

4.1 *General*
- 4.1.1 Safety Manual and Plan
- 4.1.2 Yard and Work-Force Mobilization
- 4.1.3 Qualification of Welding Procedures and Welders
  - 4.1.3.1 Structural
  - 4.1.3.2 Piping
- 4.1.4 Shop Drawings
  - 4.1.4.1 Structural
  - 4.1.4.2 Piping Isometrics
  - 4.1.4.3 Piping Spools
- 4.1.5 Receipt of Materials
- 4.1.6 QA/QC, NDT, and Dimensional Control
- 4.1.7 Weight Control Reports
- 4.1.8 As-Built Drawings and Certification Dossier

4.2 Jacket

4.2.1 Frames

    4.2.1.1   Frame 1

    4.2.1.2   Frame 2

    4.2.1.3   Frame A

    4.2.1.4   Frame B

4.2.2 Horizontal Levels

    4.2.2.1   Level 1 (EL + 10')

    4.2.2.2   Level 2

    4.2.2.3   Level 3

    4.2.2.4   Level 4

4.2.3 Appurtenances

    4.2.3.1   Disposal Pile

    4.2.3.2   Caissons

    4.2.3.3   Risers

    4.2.3.4   Boat Landing

    4.2.3.5   Corrosion Protection

    4.2.3.6   Stairs, Walkways, and Landings

4.2.4 Installation Aids

4.2.5 Loadout & Seafasten

4.3 Piling

4.3.1 Pile A1

4.3.2 Pile A2

4.3.3 Pile B1

4.3.4 Pile B2

4.3.5 Loadout & Seafasten

4.4 Topsides

4.4.1 Main Deck

    4.4.1.1   Plate Girders

    4.4.1.2   Deck Panels

    4.4.1.3   Tertiary Steel

4.4.2 Cellar Deck

    4.4.2.1   Plate Girders

    4.4.2.2   Deck Panels

    4.4.2.3   Tertiary Steel

4.4.3 Sub-Cellar Deck

4.4.4 Legs

4.4.5 Bracing

4.4.6 Equipment Installation

4.4.7 Interconnect Piping

4.4.8 Electrical

4.4.9 Instrumentation

4.4.10 Precommissioning

4.4.11 Appurtenances

    4.4.11.1   Flare Boom

    4.4.11.2   Stairs, Walkways, & Landings

    4.4.11.3   Installation Aids

4.4.12 Loadout & Seafasten

5.0 Transportation

5.1 General

    5.1.1   Safety Manual and Plan

    5.1.2   Seafastening Drawings

    5.1.3   Marine Warranty Surveyor Review and Approval

5.2 Jacket

5.3 Piling

5.4 Topsides

6.0 Installation, Hookup, and Commissioning

6.1 General

    6.1.1   Safety Manual and Plan

    6.1.2   Installation Procedures and Drawings

    6.1.3   Qualification of Welding Procedures and Welders

        6.1.3.1   Structural

        6.1.3.2   Piping

    6.1.4   As-Installed Drawings

    6.1.5   Mobilization

    6.1.6   Demobilization

6.2 Jacket

6.3 Piling

6.4 Topsides

    6.4.1   Hookup

    6.4.2   Commissioning

    6.4.3   Startup

This WBS example is illustrative only and is intended to provide guidance to the reader. No claim of completeness is made—for any specific project, the example may be complete or incomplete. As expressed previously in the *PMBOK® Guide*, "the project management team is always responsible for determining what is appropriate for any given project" (Project Management Institute 2000).

Appendix F

Environmental Management WBS Example

ENVIRONMENTAL MANAGEMENT PROJECT WBS TO CONDUCT A BIO-VENTING TEST FOR THE REMEDIATION OF HYDROCARBON IMPACTED SOILS

1.0 **System Design**
- 1.1 *Initial Design*
- 1.2 *Client Meeting*
- 1.3 *Draft Design*
- 1.4 *Client & Regulatory Agency Meeting*
- 1.5 *Final Design*

2.0 **System Installation**
- 2.1 *Facility Planning Meeting*
- 2.2 *Well Installation*
- 2.3 *Electrical Power Drop Installation*
- 2.4 *Blower and Piping Installation*

3.0 **Soil Permeability Test**
- 3.1 *System Operation Check*
- 3.2 *Soil Permeability Test*
- 3.3 *Test Report*

4.0 **Initial In Situ Respiration Test**
- 4.1 *In Situ Respiration Test*
- 4.2 *Test Report*

5.0 Long-Term Bio-Venting Test

    5.1 Ambient Air Monitoring

    5.2 Operation, Maintenance, and Monitoring

    5.3 Three-Month In Situ Respiration Test

    5.4 Test Report

    5.5 6 month In Situ Respiration Test

    5.6 Test Report

6.0 Confirmation Sampling

    6.1 Soil Boring and Sampling

    6.2 Data Validation

7.0 Report Preparation

    7.1 Pre-Draft Report

    7.2 Client Meeting

    7.3 Draft Report

    7.4 Client & Regulatory Agency Meeting

    7.5 Final Report

8.0 Project Management

    8.1 Project Plan Development

    8.2 Project Plan Execution

    8.3 Overall Change Control

This WBS example is illustrative only and is intended to provide guidance to the reader. No claim of completeness is made—for any specific project, the example may be complete or incomplete. As expressed previously in the *PMBOK® Guide*, "the project management team is always responsible for determining what is appropriate for any given project" (Project Management Institute 2000).

Appendix G

Process Improvement WBS Example

PROCESS IMPROVEMENT PROJECT WBS

This WBS example is used with permission of the California Department of Transportation. This is an example of a WBS for a process improvement project. It is divided into three phases:

1. Research to determine the best solution to the problem. This research includes the recommendation of a solution, or solutions, to the sponsor.

2. Implementation of the approved solution(s). If there were more than one approved solution, then the "Phase 2" WBS would be repeated for each solution.

3. Evaluation to determine if the solution works. This leads back to further research and continuous process improvement.

1.0   Phase 1: Research and recommendations

    1.1   Phase 1 Charter

    1.2   Project Management Plans for Phase 1

        1.2.1   Scope Management

        1.2.2   Cost and Schedule Management

        1.2.3   Quality Management

        1.2.4   Human Resources Management

        1.2.5   Communication Management

        1.2.6   Risk Management

        1.2.7   Procurement Management

    1.3   Research

        1.3.1   Documentation of the "State of the Art"

            1.3.1.1   Document Search

            1.3.1.2   Consultation with Experts

            1.3.1.3   Benchmarking

            1.3.1.4   Product and Software Review

      1.3.2   Documentation of the Current State in the Subject
            Organization
            1.3.2.1   Interviews
            1.3.2.2   Surveys
            1.3.2.3   Statistical Analysis
            1.3.2.4   Flow Charts of Current Processes

1.4 *Identification of Improvement Needs*
      1.4.1   Determination of Desired State (Vision Statement)
      1.4.2   Gap Analysis
      1.4.3   Most Likely Solutions
            1.4.3.1   Brainstorming
            1.4.3.2   Statistical Analysis
            1.4.3.3   Flow Charts of Desired Processes

1.5 *Recommendations*
      1.5.1   Recommendation 1
            1.5.1.1   Draft Charter
            1.5.1.2   Estimated Cost
      1.5.2   Recommendation 2
            1.5.2.1   Draft Charter
            1.5.2.2   Estimated Cost
      1.5.3   Recommendation n
            1.5.3.1   Draft Charter
            1.5.3.2   Estimated Cost

2.0 Phase 2: Implementation of Approved Recommendation x
(this portion of the WBS is repeated for each approved recommendation)

2.1 *Recommendation x Charter*
(approved and amended version of the draft from 1.5)

2.2 *Project Management Plans for Phase 2*
(seven plans, as for Phase 1)

2.3 *Process Documentation*
      2.3.1   Draft process (policy, handbook, manual chapter, etc.)
      2.3.2   Review
      2.3.3   Revision (2.3.2 and 2.3.3 are iterative—repeat until there is
            consensus)
      2.3.4   Publication
            2.3.4.1   Hardcopy
            2.3.4.2   Internet or Intranet
            2.3.4.3   Other

2.4 *Tools (software, etc.)*
      2.4.1   Design
      2.4.2   Build
      2.4.3   Test
      2.4.4   Revision (2.4.3 and 2.4.4 are iterative—repeat until the
            product meets its goals)
      2.4.5   Implementation

2.5 *Training*

    2.5.1   Instructors
        2.5.1.1 Hiring
        2.5.1.2 Training ("Train the Trainers")
    2.5.2   Development
        2.5.2.1 Draft Training Materials
        2.5.2.2 Review and Pilot
        2.5.2.3 Revision (2.5.2.2 and 2.5.2.3 are iterative—repeat until the class meets its goals)
    2.5.3   Delivery

3.0 Phase 3: Evaluation

3.1 *Project Management Plans for Phase 3*
(seven plans, as for Phase 1)

3.2 *Documentation of the New State in the Subject Organization*

    3.2.1   Interviews
    3.2.2   Surveys
    3.2.3   Statistical Analysis
    3.2.4   Flow Charts of New Processes

3.3 *Identification of Deficiencies*

    3.3.1   Flow Charts of desired processes (from 1.4.3.3)
    3.3.2   Gap Analysis

3.4 *Recommendations for New Projects*

    3.4.1   Recommendation 1
        3.4.1.1 Draft Charter
        3.4.1.2 Estimated Cost
    3.4.2   Recommendation 2
        3.4.2.1 Draft Charter
        3.4.2.2 Estimated Cost
    3.4.3   Recommendation n
        3.4.3.1 Draft Charter
        3.4.3.2 Estimated Cost

This WBS example is illustrative only and is intended to provide guidance to the reader. No claim of completeness is made—for any specific project, the example may be complete or incomplete. As expressed previously in the *PMBOK® Guide*, "the project management team is always responsible for determining what is appropriate for any given project" (Project Management Institute 2000).

Appendix H

Pharmaceutical WBS Example

PHARMACEUTICAL PROJECT WBS

The following represents an example of a WBS for a pharmaceutical development project. It is not intended to represent the only feasible WBS for this type of project. There are numerous variations and approaches that a project manager can take to develop the WBS for the project. This example represents the new compound. Level 1 illustrates the various phases of pharmaceutical development. Level 2 represents the functional area work packages per each phase of pharmaceutical development. Level 3 represents standard sub-work packages for each of the functional areas. For consistency sake, these sub-work packages have used "carried forward" for each phase of the pharmaceutical development. In reality, many of these sub-work packages are specific to a given phase of development. They were carried forward to illustrate a consistent level of detail for this example.

It is recommended that the project manager develop the WBS to a level of detail that is appropriate for him/her and his/her team. For example, if a new project is a line extension of an existing project, it is likely that the project manager may choose to not include any aspect of lead identification in the WBS. Additionally, the project manager may want to illustrate geographic components in the WBS that would necessitate a modification to what is depicted here.

The graphical depiction of the WBS covers the first two levels of the WBS. The tabular depiction of the WBS covers the three levels. The project manager may choose to add levels to the WBS to adequately detail the work packages for the project team.

Pharmaceutical Work Breakdown Structure Example

New Compcund

Lead Identification Program 1
- Discovery Support 1.1
- Tox/ADME Support 1.2
- Medical Support 1.3
- Clin Pharm Support 1.4
- CM&C Support 1.5
- Marketing/Sales Support 1.6
- Regulatory Support 1.7
- Legal Support 1.8
- Project Mgmt. Support 1.9

Preclinical Program 2
- Discovery Support 2.1
- Tox/ADME Support 2.2
- Medical Support 2.3
- Clin Pharm Support 2.4
- CM&C Support 2.5
- Marketing/Sales Support 2.6
- Regulatory Support 2.7
- Legal Support 2.8
- Project Mgmt. Support 2.9

Phase I Program 3
- Discovery Support 3.1
- Tox/ADME Support 3.2
- Medical Support 3.3
- Clin Pharm Support 3.4
- CM&C Support 3.5
- Marketing/Sales Support 3.6
- Regulatory Support 3.7
- Legal Support 3.8
- Project Mgmt. Support 3.9

Phase II Program 4
- Discovery Support 4.1
- Tox/ADME Support 4.2
- Medical Support 4.3
- Clin Pharm Support 4.4
- CM&C Support 4.5
- Marketing/Sales Support 4.6
- Regulatory Support 4.7
- Legal Support 4.8
- Project Mgmt. Support 4.9

Phase III Program 5
- Discovery Support 5.1
- Tox/ADME Support 5.2
- Medical Support 5.3
- Clin Pharm Support 5.4
- CM&C Support 5.5
- Marketing/Sales Support 5.6
- Regulatory Support 5.7
- Legal Support 5.8
- Project Mgmt. Support 5.9

Submission/Launch Phase 6
- Discovery Support 6.1
- Tox/ADME Support 6.2
- Medical Support 6.3
- Clin Pharm Support 6.4
- CM&C Support 6.5
- Marketing/Sales Support 6.6
- Regulatory Support 6.7
- Legal Support 6.8
- Project Mgmt. Support 6.9

Phase IV Commercial Program 7
- Discovery Support 7.1
- Tox/ADME Support 7.2
- Medical Support 7.3
- Clin Pharm Support 7.4
- CM&C Support 7.5
- Marketing/Sales Support 7.6
- Regulatory Support 7.7
- Legal Support 7.8
- Project Mgmt. Support 7.9

©2001 Project Management Institute, Four Campus Boulevard, Newtown Square, PA 19073-3299 USA

NEW COMPOUND
Lead Identification Program   **1**

Discovery Support   *1.1*

     Hypothesis Generation   1.1.1

     Assay Screening   1.1.2

     Lead Optimization   1.1.3

     Other Discovery Support   1.1.4

Tox/ADME Support   *1.2*

     Non-GLP Animal Studies   1.2.1

     Bioanalytical Assay Development   1.2.2

     ADME Evaluations   1.2.3

     Acute Toxicological Studies   1.2.4

     Sub-Chronic Toxicological Studies   1.2.5

     Chronic Toxicological Studies   1.2.6

     Other Tox/ADME Support   1.2.7

Medical Support   *1.3*

     Pharmacokinetic/Pharmacodynamic Study(ies)   1.3.1

     Dose Ranging Study(ies)   1.3.2

     Multiple Dose Safety Study(ies)   1.3.3

     Multiple Dose Efficacy Study(ies)   1.3.4

     Pivotal Registration Study(ies)   1.3.5

     Other Clinical Study(ies)   1.3.6

Clinical Pharmacology Support   *1.4*

     Pharmacokinetic Study(ies)   1.4.1

     Drug Interaction Study(ies)   1.4.2

     Renal Effect Study(ies)   1.4.3

     Hepatic Effect Study(ies)   1.4.4

     Bioequivalency Study(ies)   1.4.5

     Other Clinical Pharmacology Study(ies)   1.4.6

CM&C Support   *1.5*

     Active Pharmaceutical Ingredient Development
Program   1.5.1

     New Drug Product Development Program   1.5.2

     Clinical Trial Supply Program   1.5.3

     Active Pharmaceutical Ingredient Tech Transfer/
Validation/Launch Program   1.5.4

     New Drug Product Tech Transfer/Validation/
Launch Program   1.5.5

     Other CM&C Support   1.5.6

Marketing/Sales Support   *1.6*

     Market Research Program   1.6.1

     Branding Program   1.6.2

     Pricing Program   1.6.3

     Sales Development Program   1.6.4

     Other Marketing/Sales Support   1.6.5

Regulatory Support   *1.7*

     Preclinical Package   1.7.1

     Clinical Package   1.7.2

     Clinical Pharmacology Package   1.7.3

     CM&C Package   1.7.4

     Promotional Materials Package   1.7.5

Other Regulatory Support	1.7.6
Legal Support	*1.8*
Publications	1.8.1
Patents/Intellectual Property	1.8.2
Trademarks	1.8.3
Other Legal Support	1.8.4
Project Management Support	*1.9*
Compound Project Management	1.9.1
Preclinical Project Management	1.9.2
Clinical Project Management	1.9.3
CM&C Project Management	1.9.4
Other Project Management Support	1.9.5

Preclinical Program	**2**
Discovery Support	*2.1*
Hypothesis Generation	2.1.1
Assay Screening	2.1.2
Lead Optimization	2.1.3
Other Discovery Support	2.1.4
Tox/ADME Support	*2.2*
Non-GLP Animal Studies	2.2.1
Bioanalytical Assay Development	2.2.2
ADME Evaluations	2.2.3
Acute Toxicological Studies	2.2.4
Sub Chronic Toxicological Studies	2.2.5
Chronic Toxicological Studies	2.2.6
Other Tox/ADME Support	2.2.7
Medical Support	*2.3*
Pharmacokinetic/Pharmacodynamic Study(ies)	2.3.1
Dose Ranging Study(ies)	2.3.2
Multiple Dose Safety Study(ies)	2.3.3
Multiple Dose Efficacy Study(ies)	2.3.4
Pivotal Registration Study(ies)	2.3.5
Other Clinical Study(ies)	2.3.6
Clinical Pharmacology Support	*2.4*
Pharmacokinetic Study(ies)	2.4.1
Drug Interaction Study(ies)	2.4.2
Renal Effect Study(ies)	2.4.3
Hepatic Effect Study(ies)	2.4.4
Bioequivalency Study(ies)	2.4.5
Other Clinical Pharmacology Study(ies)	2.4.6
CM&C Support	*2.5*
Active Pharmaceutical Ingredient Development Program	2.5.1
New Drug Product Development Program	2.5.2
Clinical Trial Supply Program	2.5.3
Active Pharmaceutical Ingredient Tech Transfer/ Validation/Launch Program	2.5.4
New Drug Product Tech Transfer/Validation/ Launch Program	2.5.5
Other CM&C Support	2.5.6

Marketing/Sales Support	*2.6*
Market Research Program	2.6.1
Branding Program	2.6.2
Pricing Program	2.6.3
Sales Development Program	2.6.4
Other Marketing/Sales Support	2.6.5
Regulatory Support	*2.7*
Preclinical Package	2.7.1
Clinical Package	2.7.2
Clinical Pharmacology Package	2.7.3
CM&C Package	2.7.4
Promotional Materials Package	2.7.5
Other Regulatory Support	2.7.6
Legal Support	*2.8*
Publications	2.8.1
Patents/Intellectual Property	2.8.2
Trademarks	2.8.3
Other Legal Support	2.8.4
Project Management Support	*2.9*
Compound Project Management	2.9.1
Preclinical Project Management	2.9.2
Clinical Project Management	2.9.3
CM&C Project Management	2.9.4
Other Project Management Support	2.9.5
Phase I Program	**3**
Discovery Support	*3.1*
Hypothesis Generation	3.1.1
Assay Screening	3.1.2
Lead Optimization	3.1.3
Other Discovery Support	3.1.4
Tox/ADME Support	*3.2*
Non-GLP Animal Studies	3.2.1
Bioanalytical Assay Development	3.2.2
ADME Evaluations	3.2.3
Acute Toxicological Studies	3.2.4
Sub-Chronic Toxicological Studies	3.2.5
Chronic Toxicological Studies	3.2.6
Other Tox/ADME Support	3.2.7
Medical Support	*3.3*
Pharmacokinetic/Pharmacodynamic Study(ies)	3.3.1
Dose Ranging Study(ies)	3.3.2
Multiple Dose Safety Study(ies)	3.3.3
Multiple Dose Efficacy Study(ies)	3.3.4
Pivotal Registration Study(ies)	3.3.5
Other Clinical Study(ies)	3.3.6
Clinical Pharmacology Support	*3.4*
Pharmacokinetic Study(ies)	3.4.1
Drug Interaction Study(ies)	3.4.2
Renal Effect Study(ies)	3.4.3
Hepatic Effect Study(ies)	3.4.4
Bioequivalency Study(ies)	3.4.5
Other Clinical Pharmacology Study(ies)	3.4.6

CM&C Support	*3.5*
Active Pharmaceutical Ingredient Development Program	3.5.1
New Drug Product Development Program	3.5.2
Clinical Trial Supply Program	3.5.3
Active Pharmaceutical Ingredient Tech Transfer/ Validation/Launch Program	3.5.4
New Drug Product Tech Transfer/Validation/ Launch Program	3.5.5
Other CM&C Support	3.5.6
Marketing/Sales Support	*3.6*
Market Research Program	3.6.1
Branding Program	3.6.2
Pricing Program	3.6.3
Sales Development Program	3.6.4
Other Marketing/Sales Support	3.6.5
Regulatory Support	*3.7*
Preclinical Package	3.7.1
Clinical Package	3.7.2
Clinical Pharmacology Package	3.7.3
CM&C Package	3.7.4
Promotional Materials Package	3.7.5
Other Regulatory Support	3.7.6
Legal Support	*3.8*
Publications	3.8.1
Patents/Intellectual Property	3.8.2
Trademarks	3.8.3
Other Legal Support	3.8.4
Project Management Support	*3.9*
Compound Project Management	3.9.1
Preclinical Project Management	3.9.2
Clinical Project Management	3.9.3
CM&C Project Management	3.9.4
Other Project Management Support	3.9.5
Phase II Program	**4**
Discovery Support	*4.1*
Hypothesis Generation	4.1.1
Assay Screening	4.1.2
Lead Optimization	4.1.3
Other Discovery Support	4.1.4
Tox/ADME Support	*4.2*
Non-GLP Animal Studies	4.2.1
Bioanalytical Assay Development	4.2.2
ADME Evaluations	4.2.3
Acute Toxicological Studies	4.2.4
Sub-Chronic Toxicological Studies	4.2.5
Chronic Toxicological Studies	4.2.6
Other Tox/ADME Support	4.2.7
Medical Support	*4.3*
Pharmacokinetic/Pharmacodynamic Study(ies)	4.3.1
Dose Ranging Study(ies)	4.3.2
Multiple Dose Safety Study(ies)	4.3.3

Multiple Dose Efficacy Study(ies)	4.3.4
Pivotal Registration Study(ies)	4.3.5
Other Clinical Study(ies)	4.3.6
Clinical Pharmacology Support	*4.4*
Pharmacokinetic Study(ies)	4.4.1
Drug Interaction Study(ies)	4.4.2
Renal Effect Study(ies)	4.4.3
Hepatic Effect Study(ies)	4.4.4
Bioequivalency Study(ies)	4.4.5
Other Clinical Pharmacology Study(ies)	4.4.6
CM&C Support	*4.5*
Active Pharmaceutical Ingredient Development Program	4.5.1
New Drug Product Development Program	4.5.2
Clinical Trial Supply Program	4.5.3
Active Pharmaceutical Ingredient Tech Transfer/ Validation/Launch Program	4.5.4
New Drug Product Tech Transfer/Validation/ Launch Program	4.5.5
Other CM&C Support	4.5.6
Marketing/Sales Support	*4.6*
Market Research Program	4.6.1
Branding Program	4.6.2
Pricing Program	4.6.3
Sales Development Program	4.6.4
Other Marketing/Sales Support	4.6.5
Regulatory Support	*4.7*
Preclinical Package	4.7.1
Clinical Package	4.7.2
Clinical Pharmacology Package	4.7.3
CM&C Package	4.7.4
Promotional Materials Package	4.7.5
Other Regulatory Support	4.7.6
Legal Support	*4.8*
Publications	4.8.1
Patents/Intellectual Property	4.8.2
Trademarks	4.8.3
Other Legal Support	4.8.4
Project Management Support	*4.9*
Compound Project Management	4.9.1
Preclinical Project Management	4.9.2
Clinical Project Management	4.9.3
CM&C Project Management	4.9.4
Other Project Management Support	4.9.5
Phase III Program	**5**
Discovery Support	*5.1*
Hypothesis Generation	5.1.1
Assay Screening	5.1.2
Lead Optimization	5.1.3
Other Discovery Support	5.1.4

Tox/ADME Support	*5.2*
Non-GLP Animal Studies	5.2.1
Bioanalytical Assay Development	5.2.2
ADME Evaluations	5.2.3
Acute Toxicological Studies	5.2.4
Sub-chronic Toxicological Studies	5.2.5
Chronic Toxicological Studies	5.2.6
Other Tox/ADME Support	5.2.7
Medical Support	*5.3*
Pharmacokinetic/Pharmacodynamic Study(ies)	5.3.1
Dose Ranging Study(ies)	5.3.2
Multiple Dose Safety Study(ies)	5.3.3
Multiple Dose Efficacy Study(ies)	5.3.4
Pivotal Registration Study(ies)	5.3.5
Other Clinical Study(ies)	5.3.6
Clinical Pharmacology Support	*5.4*
Pharmacokinetic Study(ies)	5.4.1
Drug Interaction Study(ies)	5.4.2
Renal Effect Study(ies)	5.4.3
Hepatic Effect Study(ies)	5.4.4
Bioequivalency Study(ies)	5.4.5
Other Clinical Pharmacology Study(ies)	5.4.6
CM&C Support	*5.5*
Active Pharmaceutical Ingredient Development Program	5.5.1
New Drug Product Development Program	5.5.2
Clinical Trial Supply Program	5.5.3
Active Pharmaceutical Ingredient Tech Transfer/Validation/Launch Program	5.5.4
New Drug Product Tech Transfer/Validation/Launch Program	5.5.5
Other CM&C Support	5.5.6
Marketing/Sales Support	*5.6*
Market Research Program	5.6.1
Branding Program	5.6.2
Pricing Program	5.6.3
Sales Development Program	5.6.4
Other Marketing/Sales Support	5.6.5
Regulatory Support	*5.7*
Preclinical Package	5.7.1
Clinical Package	5.7.2
Clinical Pharmacology Package	5.7.3
CM&C Package	5.7.4
Promotional Materials Package	5.7.5
Other Regulatory Support	5.7.6
Legal Support	*5.8*
Publications	5.8.1
Patents/Intellectual Property	5.8.2
Trademarks	5.8.3
Other Legal Support	5.8.4

Project Management Support	*5.9*
Compound Project Management	5.9.1
Preclinical Project Management	5.9.2
Clinical Project Management	5.9.3
CM&C Project Management	5.9.4
Other Project Management Support	5.9.5
Submission/Launch Phase	**6**
Discovery Support	*6.1*
Hypothesis Generation	6.1.1
Assay Screening	6.1.2
Lead Optimization	6.1.3
Other Discovery Support	6.1.4
Tox/ADME Support	*6.2*
Non-GLP Animal Studies	6.2.1
Bioanalytical Assay Development	6.2.2
ADME Evaluations	6.2.3
Acute Toxicological Studies	6.2.4
Sub-Chronic Toxicological Studies	6.2.5
Chronic Toxicological Studies	6.2.6
Other Tox/ADME Support	6.2.7
Medical Support	*6.3*
Pharmacokinetic/Pharmacodynamic Study(ies)	6.3.1
Dose Ranging Study(ies)	6.3.2
Multiple Dose Safety Study(ies)	6.3.3
Multiple Dose Efficacy Study(ies)	6.3.4
Pivotal Registration Study(ies)	6.3.5
Other Clinical Study(ies)	6.3.6
Clinical Pharmacology Support	*6.4*
Pharmacokinetic Study(ies)	6.4.1
Drug Interaction Study(ies)	6.4.2
Renal Effect Study(ies)	6.4.3
Hepatic Effect Study(ies)	6.4.4
Bioequivalency Study(ies)	6.4.5
Other Clinical Pharmacology Study(ies)	6.4.6
CM&C Support	*6.5*
Active Pharmaceutical Ingredient Development Program	6.5.1
New Drug Product Development Program	6.5.2
Clinical Trial Supply Program	6.5.3
Active Pharmaceutical Ingredient Tech Transfer/ Validation/Launch Program	6.5.4
New Drug Product Tech Transfer/Validation/ Launch Program	6.5.5
Other CM&C Support	6.5.6
Marketing/Sales Support	*6.6*
Market Research Program	6.6.1
Branding Program	6.6.2
Pricing Program	6.6.3
Sales Development Program	6.6.4
Other Marketing/Sales Support	6.6.5

Regulatory Support	*6.7*
Preclinical Package	6.7.1
Clinical Package	6.7.2
Clinical Pharmacology Package	6.7.3
CM&C Package	6.7.4
Promotional Materials Package	6.7.5
Other Regulatory Support	6.7.6
Legal Support	*6.8*
Publications	6.8.1
Patents/Intellectual Property	6.8.2
Trademarks	6.8.3
Other Legal Support	6.8.4
Project Management Support	*6.9*
Compound Project Management	6.9.1
Preclinical Project Management	6.9.2
Clinical Project Management	6.9.3
CM&C Project Management	6.9.4
Other Project Management Support	6.9.5

Phase IV/Commercialization Program — 7

Discovery Support	*7.1*
Hypothesis Generation	7.1.1
Assay Screening	7.1.2
Lead Optimization	7.1.3
Other Discovery Support	7.1.4
Tox/ADME Support	*7.2*
Non-GLP Animal Studies	7.2.1
Bioanalytical Assay Development	7.2.2
ADME Evaluations	7.2.3
Acute Toxicological Studies	7.2.4
Sub-Chronic Toxicological Studies	7.2.5
Chronic Toxicological Studies	7.2.6
Other Tox/ADME Support	7.2.7
Medical Support	*7.3*
Pharmacokinetic/Pharmacodynamic Study(ies)	7.3.1
Dose Ranging Study(ies)	7.3.2
Multiple Dose Safety Study(ies)	7.3.3
Multiple Dose Efficacy Study(ies)	7.3.4
Pivotal Registration Study(ies)	7.3.5
Other Clinical Study(ies)	7.3.6
Clinical Pharmacology Support	*7.4*
Pharmacokinetic Study(ies)	7.4.1
Drug Interaction Study(ies)	7.4.2
Renal Effect Study(ies)	7.4.3
Hepatic Effect Study(ies)	7.4.4
Bioequivalency Study(ies)	7.4.5
Other Clinical Pharmacology Study(ies)	7.4.6
CM&C Support	*7.5*
Active Pharmaceutical Ingredient Development Program	7.5.1
New Drug Product Development Program	7.5.2
Clinical Trial Supply Program	7.5.3
Active Pharmaceutical Ingredient Tech Transfer/ Validation/Launch Program	7.5.4

New Drug Product Tech Transfer/Validation/ Launch Program	7.5.5
Other CM&C Support	7.5.6
Marketing/Sales Support	*7.6*
Market Research Program	7.6.1
Branding Program	7.6.2
Pricing Program	7.6.3
Sales Development Program	7.6.4
Other Marketing/Sales Support	7.6.5
Regulatory Support	*7.7*
Preclinical Package	7.7.1
Clinical Package	7.7.2
Clinical Pharmacology Package	7.7.3
CM&C Package	7.7.4
Promotional Materials Package	7.7.5
Other Regulatory Support	7.7.6
Legal Support	*7.8*
Publications	7.8.1
Patents/Intellectual Property	7.8.2
Trademarks	7.8.3
Other Legal Support	7.8.4
Project Management Support	*7.9*
Compound Project Management	7.9.1
Preclinical Project Management	7.9.2
Clinical Project Management	7.9.3
CM&C Project Management	7.9.4
Other Project Management Support	7.9.5

This WBS example is illustrative only and is intended to provide guidance to the reader. No claim of completeness is made—for any specific project, the example may be complete or incomplete. As expressed previously in the *PMBOK® Guide*, "the project management team is always responsible for determining what is appropriate for any given project" (Project Management Institute 2000).

Appendix I

Process Plant Construction WBS Example

PROCESS PLANT CONSTRUCTION PROJECT WBS

PMI Project Management Standards Open Working Session volunteers at PMI's '99 Seminars & Symposium created this construction WBS example. It is an example of an engineering-oriented WBS, rather than a contractor-oriented WBS, as the orientation is on the design of systems rather than on the startup and commissioning of systems. Communication between the engineering team and the construction/commissioning team needs to be very good to minimize problems during construction. In practice there can be problems when Engineers do design based on "Systems," while the Crafts/Trades (Contractors) do their work by location and sequence.

However, it should be noted that whether the WBS has a process focus, a systems focus, a structure focus, or some other focus, the sequence of work is not the primary objective. The issue is whether the work required to complete the desired outcome and meet the project objectives has been captured in enough detail to identify resources, assign responsibility, and set sequence.

1.0 System Design
- *1.1 System Engineering*
- *1.2 Site Development*
- *1.3 Civil Structures*
- *1.4 Thermal Systems*
- *1.5 Flow Systems*
- *1.6 Storage Systems*
- *1.7 Electrical Systems*
- *1.8 Mechanical Systems*

1.9 Environmental Systems

1.10 Instrumentation & Control Systems

1.11 Auxiliary Systems

2.0 Construction

2.1 Site Development

2.2 Civil Structures

2.3 Thermal Systems

2.4 Flow Systems

2.5 Storage Systems

2.6 Electrical Systems

2.7 Mechanical Systems

2.8 Instrument & Control Systems

2.9 Environmental Systems

2.10 Temporary Structure

2.11 Auxiliary Systems

3.0 Legal & Regulatory

3.1 Licensing (non-government)/Permitting (government)

3.2 Environmental Impact

3.3 Labor Agreements

3.4 Land Acquisition

3.5 Other Legal/Regulatory Requirements

4.0 Project Management

4.1 Project Plan Development

4.2 Status Reports

4.3 Data Management

4.4 Configuration Management

4.5 Meetings (Minutes)

4.6 Contract Administration

5.0 System Test/Startup

Note: PMI Project Management Standards Open Working Session volunteers at PMI's '99 Seminars & Symposium created this WBS example.

This WBS example is illustrative only and is intended to provide guidance to the reader. No claim of completeness is made—for any specific project, the example may be complete or incomplete. As expressed previously in the *PMBOK® Guide*, "the project management team is always responsible for determining what is appropriate for any given project" (Project Management Institute 2000).

Appendix J

Service Industry Outsourcing WBS Example

SERVICE INDUSTRY OUTSOURCING PROJECT WBS

The really unique aspect of this WBS is its inclusion of an RFP process.

1.0 Needs Analysis

    1.1 Determine Need for Service

    1.2 Define & Baseline Requirements

    1.3 Develop Specifications

    1.4 Develop High-Level Statement of Work

2.0 Market Analysis

    2.1 Determine Internal Capability + Cost

    2.2 Identify Qualified Vendors

    2.3 Prepare RFI (Information)

    2.4 Evaluate RFI Submissions

    2.5 Conduct Decision Analysis (includes make/buy)

3.0 RFP Development

    3.1 Develop Solution Criteria

    3.2 Finalize Requirements

    3.3 Finalize Schedule

    3.4 Finalize Budget

4.0 Solicitation

 4.1 Issue RFQ

 4.2 Issue RFP

 4.3 Receive Bids

 4.4 Evaluate Response

 4.5 Qualify Vendors

 4.6 Award/Select Vendors

 4.7 Issue LOI(s)

5.0 Contract

 5.1 Develop Master Agreement

  5.1.1   Negotiate Contract

  5.1.2   Finalize Terms & Conditions (use boiler plate)

  5.1.3   Finalize Scope/Schedule/Cost

 5.2 Develop Contract Orders/Task Orders/CSOWs

  5.2.1   Develop Specific Deliverables

  5.2.2   Identify Resources

  5.2.3   Define SLAs

  5.2.4   Define Acceptance Criteria

  5.2.5   Define Performance Measures

  5.2.6   Issue PO/Task Order

 5.3 Execute Agreement/Signed Contract

6.0 Services Perspective

 6.1 Contract Order SOW

 6.2 Task Order SOW

Note: PMI Project Management Standards Open Working Session volunteers at PMI's '99 Seminars & Symposium created this WBS example.

This WBS example is illustrative only and is intended to provide guidance to the reader. No claim of completeness is made—for any specific project, the example may be complete or incomplete. As expressed previously in the *PMBOK® Guide*, "the project management team is always responsible for determining what is appropriate for any given project" (Project Management Institute 2000).

Appendix K

Web Design WBS Example

WEB DESIGN PROJECT WBS

Goal: Design an Internet site that sells products within one country.

Assumption: This project is being conducted internally to develop a commerce site to sell the company's own products. The company will create and host the design.

1.0 Web Design

    1.1 Web Design Methods

        1.1.1   Evaluate Available Web Design Methods

        1.1.2   Select Web Design Method

    1.2 Web Designer

        1.2.1   Hire Web Designer

        1.2.2   Educate Web Designer

    1.3 Web Site Design

        1.3.1   Consult Web Design Expert

        1.3.2   Decide on Web Site Design

    1.4 Web Site Programs

        1.4.1   Validate Web Site in Conformance to Internal Business Process

        1.4.2   Validate Web Site in Conformance to External Requirements

        1.4.3   Approve Solution

2.0 Hardware

   2.1 Determine Sizing

   2.2 Define Hardware Architecture

   2.3 Buy Hardware

   2.4 Install Hardware

   2.5 Test Hardware

3.0 Software

   3.1 Obtain and Train Programmers

   3.2 Design Programs

   3.3 Conduct Program Peer Review

   3.4 Prototype Programs

   3.5 Order Entry
      3.5.1 Code Order Entry
      3.5.2 Test Order Entry

   3.6 Order Fulfillment
      3.6.1 Code Order Fulfillment
      3.6.2 Test Order Fulfillment

   3.7 Acknowledgment
      3.7.1 Code Acknowledgment
      3.7.2 Test Acknowledgment

   3.8 Invoicing

   3.9 Database
      3.9.1 Design Database
      3.9.2 Build Database
      3.9.3 Cleanse Data
      3.9.4 Load Database

   3.10 Test SQL

4.0 Communication

   4.1 Choose ISP

   4.2 Choose Telecom Vendor

   4.3 Define Network Environment

   4.4 Select Communication Method to Infrastructure Vendor

   4.5 Firewall & Encryption Security

5.0 Integration

    5.1 Install Software Application on Hardware

    5.2 Middleware/Application Test

    5.3 External Network Test

    5.4 Performance System Test

6.0 Logistics

    6.1 Order Processing Link

        6.1.1   Invoice Link

        6.1.2   Replenishment/Forecast Link

    6.2 Shipping Link

    6.3 Customer Support Link

    6.4 Link to Credit Authorization

Note: PMI Project Management Standards Open Working Session volunteers at PMI's '99 Seminars & Symposium created this WBS example.

This WBS example is illustrative only and is intended to provide guidance to the reader. No claim of completeness is made—for any specific project, the example may be complete or incomplete. As expressed previously in the *PMBOK® Guide*, "the project management team is always responsible for determining what is appropriate for any given project" (Project Management Institute 2000).

Appendix L

Telecom WBS Example

TELECOM PROJECT WBS

1.0 **Concept/Feasibility**
   1.1 *Develop Concept/Marketing Plan*
   1.2 *Conduct Market Analysis & Scope*
   1.3 *Conduct Technical Analysis*
   1.4 *Develop Prototype*
   1.5 *Prepare Product Development Plan/Cost/Schedule*

2.0 **Requirements**
   2.1 *Develop End-User Requirements*
   2.2 *Develop Application Requirements*
   2.3 *Develop Infrastructure (Systems) Requirements*
   2.4 *Develop Operations/Maintenance Requirements*
   2.5 *Develop Service Requirements*

3.0 **Decision**
   3.1 *Present Prototype*
   3.2 *Present Financial & Schedule*
   3.3 *Present Technical Capabilities*
   3.4 *Obtain Financial Commitment*
   3.5 *Go/No-Go Decision (Milestone)*

4.0 **Development**
   4.1 *Develop End-User Systems*
   4.2 *Develop Application*
   4.3 *Develop Infrastructure Systems & Network*

    4.4 Develop Operations/Maintenance Structure

    4.5 Develop Service Plan

5.0 Test

    5.1 Develop Test Plans for Each Aspect/Element

    5.2 Conduct Tests

    5.3 Validate Results

    5.4 Perform Corrective Action (as necessary)

    5.5 Conduct Retesting

    5.6 Revalidate Results

6.0 Deploy

    6.1 Conduct Trial in a Non-Penalty Environment

    6.2 Conduct First Live Test in First Action Site

    6.3 Complete Deployment

7.0 Life-Cycle Support

    7.1 Conduct Customer Training & Education

    7.2 Perform Turnover to Customer

    7.3 Obtain Customer Acceptance

    7.4 Perform Support & Maintenance

Note: PMI Project Management Standards Open Working Session volunteers at PMI's '99 Seminars & Symposium created this WBS example.

This WBS example is illustrative only and is intended to provide guidance to the reader. No claim of completeness is made—for any specific project, the example may be complete or incomplete. As expressed previously in the *PMBOK® Guide*, "the project management team is always responsible for determining what is appropriate for any given project" (Project Management Institute 2000).

Appendix M

Refinery TurnAround WBS Example

REFINERY TURNAROUND PROJECT WBS

This is an example of a WBS for the TurnAround (T/A) of a refinery. As used on a previous project, Level 4 was treated as the lowest level of the WBS. Work orders and their associated activities rolled up under the Equipment ID (WBS Level 4). Shift status (updated every twelve hours) was reported to upper management at Level 3 for most of the turnaround.

This WBS example is illustrative only and is intended to provide guidance to the reader. No claim of completeness is made—for any specific project, the example may be complete or incomplete. As expressed previously in the *PMBOK® Guide*, "the project management team is always responsible for determining what is appropriate for any given project" (Project Management Institute 2000).

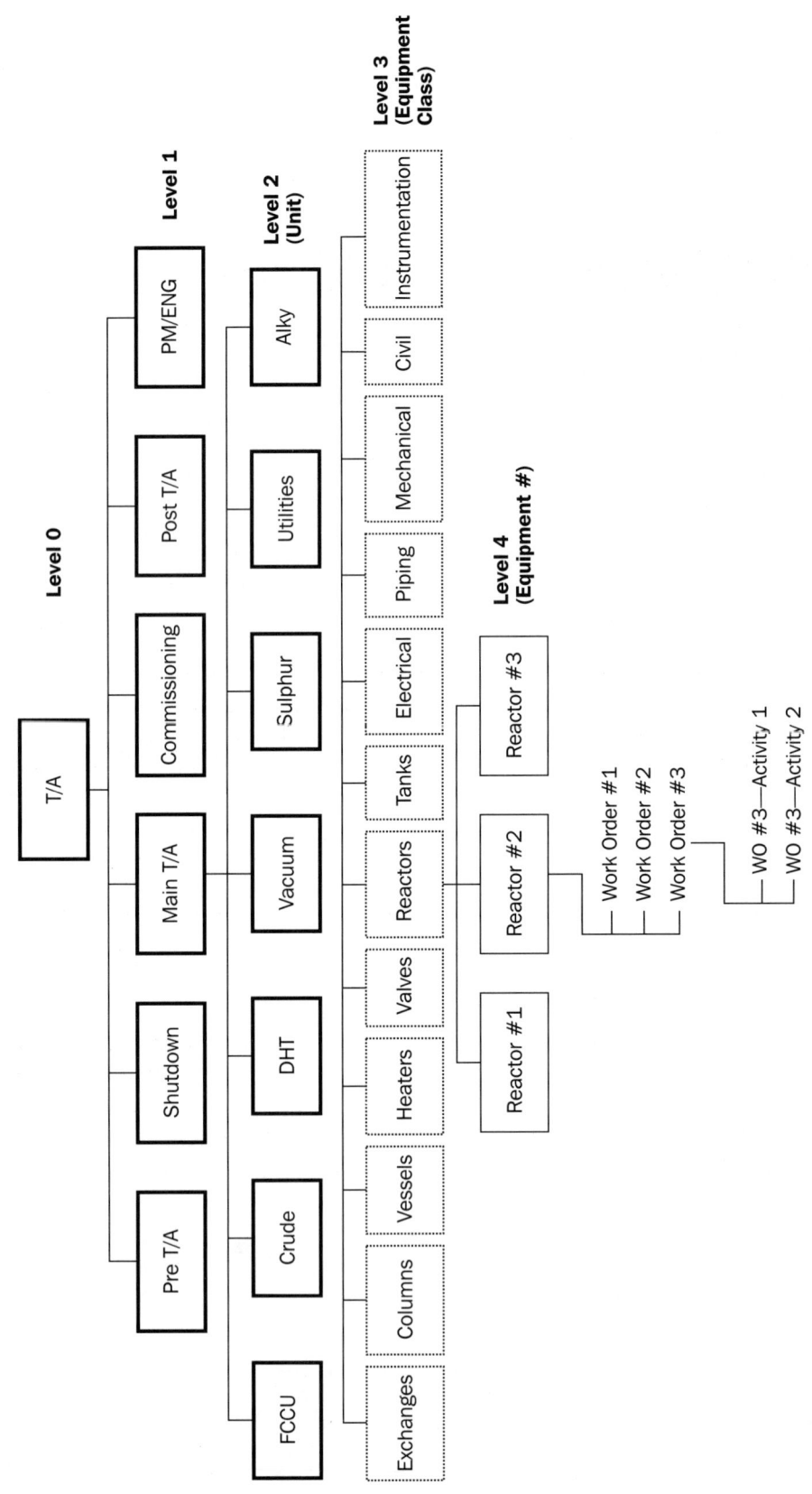

Sample WBS for Refinery T/A

Appendix N

Government Design-Bid-Build WBS Example

GOVERNMENT DESIGN-BID-BUILD PROJECT WBS

This is an example of a WBS, from the government's point of view, of a Government Design-Bid-Build Construction project. This WBS is based on the following three key assumptions.

1. Limits on the power of the executive branch of government. Every democratic system has limits of this type. The executive branch is authorized to make decisions within established limits. To proceed beyond those limits, it must obtain permission from representatives of the people. These representatives may be the legislative branch or a commission that acts for the people. Limits of this type are established no matter what system is used to appoint the chief executive. In most cases, the legislative branch appoints the chief executive (1). In some cases, the chief executive is elected directly (2).

2. Real property is obtained by eminent domain. In the private sector, developers need to own the land or have assurance that they can purchase the land before they begin the project. In the government sector, the government may begin the project long before it owns the land.

3. Of those qualified, the lowest priced bidder performs the construction. To ensure a fair competition, the government must prepare detailed plans and specifications before letting the contract.

1.0 Phase 1: Prospectus
(that which the executive branch can complete without external review or approval)

    1.1 Project Management Plans for Phase 1

        1.1.1   Scope Management Plan

        1.1.2   Cost and Schedule Management Plan

        1.1.3   Quality Management Plan

        1.1.4   Human Resources Management Plan

        1.1.5   Communication Management Plan

        1.1.6   Risk Management Plan

        1.1.7   Procurement Management Plan

    1.2 Description of Customer Needs

    1.3 Preliminary Plans of Alternatives

    1.4 Estimates for Alternatives

    1.5 Cost/Benefit Analysis

    1.6 Report

2.0 Phase 2: Selected Alternative
(may be combined with Phase 1, depending on the requirements set by the legislative branch)

    2.1 Project Management Plans for Phase 2 (seven plans, as for Phase 1)

    2.2 Environmental Studies

        2.2.1   Biological

        2.2.2   Archaeological

        2.2.3   Air Quality

        2.2.4   Water Quality

        2.2.5   Social and Economic

    2.3 More Detailed Plans of Alternatives

    2.4 Estimates for Alternatives

    2.5 Draft Report

    2.6 Final Report

3.0 Phase 3: Real Property

    3.1 Project Management Plans for Phase 3 (seven plans, as for Phase 1)

    3.2 Appraisal

    3.3 Acquisition

    3.4 Relocation of Occupants

    3.5 Demolition

    3.6 Relocation of Utilities

    3.7 Hazardous Waste Removal

    3.8 Environmental Mitigation

4.0 Phase 4: Contract Award Documents

4.1 Project Management Plans for Phase 4 (seven plans, as for Phase 1)

4.2 Detailed Plans of Selected Alternative
4.2.1 Civil Plans
4.2.2 Water Supply and Removal Plans
4.2.3 Structural Plans
4.2.4 Furnishing Plans

4.3 Specifications
4.3.1 General Provisions
4.3.2 Special Provisions

4.4 Estimate

4.5 Bid Documents

4.6 Signed Contract

5.0 Phase 5: Physical Improvement (construction)

5.1 Project Management Plans for Phase 5 (seven plans, as for Phase 1)

5.2 Civil Work
5.2.1 Earthwork
5.2.2 Pavement

5.3 Water Supply, Drainage, and Sanitation
5.3.1 Drainage
5.3.2 Water Supply
5.3.3 Sanitary Sewers and Purification

5.4 Structural Work
5.4.1 Structures
5.4.2 Electrical
5.4.3 Mechanical

5.5 Furnishings

This WBS example is illustrative only and is intended to provide guidance to the reader. No claim of completeness is made—for any specific project, the example may be complete or incomplete. As expressed previously in the *PMBOK® Guide*, "the project management team is always responsible for determining what is appropriate for any given project" (Project Management Institute 2000).

Endnotes
1. Examples: The Prime Minister in the United Kingdom, Italy, Sweden, Japan, the Netherlands, Israel, Canada, Australia, New Zealand, India, and so on; the President of South Africa; the Chancellor of Germany; City Managers, County Executives, and School Superintendents in the United States.
2. Examples: The President, Governors, and some Mayors in the United States; the President of France.

Appendix O

Software Implementation WBS Example

SOFTWARE IMPLEMENTATION PROJECT WBS

1.0 Project Management

1.1 *Planning*
- 1.1.1 Develop Project Charter
- 1.1.2 Define Scope
- 1.1.3 Develop Resource Plan
- 1.1.4 Develop Communication Plan
- 1.1.5 Develop Risk Plan
- 1.1.6 Develop Change Control Plan
- 1.1.7 Develop Quality Plan
- 1.1.8 Develop Purchase Plan
- 1.1.9 Develop Cost Plan
- 1.1.10 Develop Organization Plan
- 1.1.11 Develop Project Schedule

1.2 *Meetings*
- 1.2.1 Conduct Kickoff Meeting
- 1.2.2 Weekly Status Meeting
- 1.2.3 Monthly Tactical Meeting
- 1.2.4 Project Closing Meeting

1.3 *Administration*
- 1.3.1 Standards
  - 1.3.1.1 Document Performance Standards
  - 1.3.1.2 Document Reporting Standards
  - 1.3.1.3 Document Naming Conventions
  - 1.3.1.4 Document Housekeeping Standards
- 1.3.2 Program Office
  - 1.3.2.1 Develop Program Office Charter
  - 1.3.2.2 Assign Program Office Resources

2.0 Product Requirements

2.1 Software Requirements

2.1.1 Create Draft Software Requirements
2.1.2 Review Draft Software Requirements
2.1.3 Update Draft Software Requirements
2.1.4 Review Final Software Requirements
2.1.5 Software Requirements Approved

2.2 User Documentation

2.2.1 Create Draft User Documentation
2.2.2 Review Draft User Documentation
2.2.3 Update Draft User Documentation
2.2.4 Review Final User Documentation
2.2.5 User Documentation Approved

2.3 Training Program Materials

2.3.1 Create Initial Training Requirements
2.3.2 Review & Approve Training Requirements
2.3.3 Create Initial Training Materials
2.3.4 Review & Approve Training Materials
2.3.5 Conduct Trial Course Delivery
2.3.6 Update and Finalize Training Materials

2.4 Hardware

2.4.1 Create Draft Hardware Requirements
2.4.2 Review Draft Hardware Requirements
2.4.3 Hardware Requirements Approved

2.5 Implementation & Future Support

3.0 Detail Software Design

3.1 Create Initial Software Design

3.2 Review Initial Software Design

3.3 Update Initial Software Design

3.4 Review Final Software Design

3.5 Software Design Approved

4.0 System Construction

4.1 Configure Software

4.2 Customize User Documentation

4.3 Customize Training Program Materials

4.4 Install Hardware

4.5 Implementation & Future Support

5.0 Integration & Test

5.1 Software
5.2 System Test Plan
5.3 System Test Cases
5.4 System Test Results
5.5 Acceptance Test Plan
5.6 Acceptance Test Cases
5.7 Acceptance Test Results
5.8 User Documentation
5.9 Training Program Materials
5.10 Hardware
5.11 Implementation & Future Support

Note: PMI Project Management Standards Open Working Session volunteers at PMI's '99 Seminars & Symposium created this WBS example.

This WBS example is illustrative only and is intended to provide guidance to the reader. No claim of completeness is made—for any specific project, the example may be complete or incomplete. As expressed previously in the *PMBOK® Guide*, "the project management team is always responsible for determining what is appropriate for any given project" (Project Management Institute 2000).

Glossary

Activity: An element of work performed during the course of a project. An activity normally has an expected duration, an expected cost, and expected resource requirements. Activities can be subdivided into tasks.

Customer: The individual or group that has requested, that is the recipient, or who is paying for the deliverable(s). This could be an internal department, someone in management, an external organization, and so on.

Decomposition: Decomposition involves subdividing the major project deliverables into smaller, more manageable components until the deliverables are defined in sufficient detail to support future project activities (planning, executing, controlling, and closing).

Deliverable: Any measurable, tangible, verifiable outcome, result, or item that must be produced to complete a project or part of a project. Often used more narrowly in reference to an external deliverable, which is a deliverable that is subject to approval by the project sponsor or customer.

Organizational Breakdown Structure (OBS): A depiction of the project organization arranged so as to relate work packages to organizational units.

Phase: See Project Phase.

Project Phase: A collection of logically related project activities, usually culminating in the completion of a major deliverable.

Responsibility Assignment Matrix (RAM): A structure that relates the project organization structure to the Work Breakdown Structure to help ensure that each element of the project's scope of work is assigned to a responsible individual.

Risk Event: A discrete occurrence that may affect the project for better or worse.

Scope: The sum of the products and services to be provided as a project.

Scope Change: Any change to the project scope. A scope change almost always requires an adjustment to the project cost or schedule.

Stakeholder: Individuals and organizations that are actively involved in the project, or whose interests may be positively or negatively affected as a result of project execution or project completion. They may also exert influence over the project and its results.

Statement of Work (SOW): A narrative description of products or services to be supplied under contract.

Task: A generic term for work that is not included in the Work Breakdown Structure, but potentially could be a further decomposition of work by the individuals responsible for that work. Also, lowest level of effort on a project.

Work Breakdown Structure (WBS): A deliverable-oriented grouping of project elements that organizes and defines the total scope of the project. Each descending level represents an increasingly detailed definition of the project work.

Work Breakdown Structure (WBS) Dictionary: A document that describes each Work Breakdown Structure element, including scope, deliverable(s), specification, schedule, resource requirements, and so on.

Work Breakdown Structure (WBS) Element: An entry in the Work Breakdown Structure that can be at any level.

Work Package: A deliverable at the lowest level of the Work Breakdown Structure, when that deliverable may be assigned to another project manager to plan and execute. This may be accomplished through the use of a subproject where the work package may be further decomposed into activities.

References

Berg, Cindy, and Colenso, Kim. 2000. Work Breakdown Structure Practice Standard Project—WBS vs. Activities. *PM Network*, April.

Project Management Institute. 2000. *A Guide to the Project Management Body of Knowledge (PMBOK® Guide) – 2000 Edition.* Newtown Square, PA: Project Management Institute.

Project Management Institute. 1996. *A Guide to the Project Management Body of Knowledge (PMBOK® Guide).* Upper Darby, PA: Project Management Institute.

Raz, Tzvi, and Globerson, Shlomo. 1998. Effective Sizing and Content Definition of Work Packages. *Project Management Journal*, December.

Youker, Robert. 1990. A New Look at Work Breakdown Structure (WBS). PMI Seminars/Symposium, Calgary, Alberta, Canada.

Index

A

activity(ies)   3–4, 7, 13, 16–18, 23, 65, 75–7
assignment   3, 5, 18, 20

B

budget(s)   5, 8–9, 13, 18, 57

C

CPM Schedule   *See* schedule, Critical Path Method (CPM)
checklist(s)   11, 15
component parts   5
control   2, 4, 8, 12–13, 16, 18, 23, 31, 33–4, 38, 56, 71
cost   1, 4–9, 13–18, 20, 24, 31, 39, 40–1, 57–8, 63, 68, 71, 75
customer   4, 7, 16, 61, 64, 68, 75

D

decomposition   1, 3, 5, 14–16, 75
deliverable(s)   1, 3–6, 8–9, 12–17, 58, 75–76
diagrams   32–3

E

externally focused   1

G

Gantt chart   14

I

internally focused   1

L

level   3–5, 9, 11–18, 31, 35, 57, 65, 75–6
life-cycle   1, 9, 11, 16, 29, 64
life cycle   4, 6, 16

N

network diagram   14
number   5, 11, 15

O

OBS   *See* Organizations Breakdown Structure (OBS)
organization   1, 3, 5, 11, 14, 18–19, 21, 40–1, 71, 75
Organizational Breakdown Structure (OBS)   5, 75

P

performance   4–6, 8, 11, 13, 16, 58, 61, 71
     measurement   14, 18
phase   3, 9, 39–41, 68–9, 75

planning   1–2, 4–5, 7–8, 11–12, 14, 17–18, 31, 37, 71, 75
Precedence Diagram   14
process   1, 4, 7–8, 12–15, 17–20, 24, 29, 32, 39–40, 55, 57, 59
progress   5–6, 8–9, 13, 15, 18, 31
project management   1–2, 4–5, 8–9, 13–16, 19, 23, 29, 36, 38, 41, 56, 58, 61, 64–5, 69, 73
project scope   4–8, 11–12

R

RAM   *See* Responsibility Assignment Matrix (RAM)
reporting   6, 8–9, 13–14, 18, 71
requirements   11–12, 14, 16–18, 56–7, 59, 63, 68, 72
     resource   5, 15, 17, 23, 75–6
Responsibility Assignment Matrix (RAM)   5, 75
risk   7–9, 11, 13, 39, 68, 71
     event   16–17, 75
rolling wave planning   16

S

SME   *See* subject matter expert (SME)
SOW   *See* Statement of Work (SOW)
schedule   4–6, 8–9, 13–16, 18, 24, 33, 39, 57–8, 63, 68, 71, 76
     Critical Path Method (CPM)   14
scope   1, 3–5, 8–9, 14, 30, 58, 63, 68, 71, 75–6
     change   13
stakeholder(s)   4–6, 9, 12, 16–18, 23
Statement of Work (SOW)   12, 18, 57–8, 75
status   5–6, 9, 16, 18, 56, 65, 71
structure   1, 3, 5, 9, 13, 16, 18, 55–6, 64, 75
subject matter expert (SME)   13
subproject   4, 76

T

task(s)   14, 16, 58, 75

W

WBS   *See* Work Breakdown Structure (WBS)
Work Breakdown Structure (WBS)   1–9, 11–16, 23–4, 31, 36, 38, 40–1, 55–8, 61, 64–5, 67, 69, 73, 75–6
     dictionary   76
     element(s)   4, 5, 11–18, 76
     level of detail   18
     lower level   12
     upper level   4
work package   4, 9, 13, 43, 75–6
work products   5

Upgrade Your Project Management Knowledge
with First-Class Publications from PMI

New Books

A Guide to the Project Management Body of Knowledge (PMBOK® Guide) – 2000 Edition

PMI's *PMBOK® Guide* has become *the* essential sourcebook for the project management profession and its de facto global standard, with over 700,000 copies in circulation worldwide. This new edition incorporates numerous recommendations and changes to the 1996 edition, including: progressive elaboration is given more emphasis; the role of the project office is acknowledged; the treatment of earned value is expanded in three chapters; the linkage between organizational strategy and project management is strengthened throughout; and the chapter on risk management has been rewritten with six processes instead of four. Newly added processes, tools, and techniques are aligned with the five project management processes and nine knowledge areas. For example, reserve time, variance analysis, and activity attributes are added to Chapter 6 (Project Time Management); estimating publications and earned value measurement are added to Chapter 7 (Project Cost Management); and project reports, project presentations, and project closure are added to Chapter 10 (Project Communications Management). This is one publication you'll want to have for quick reference both at work and at home.

ISBN: 1-880410-23-0 (paperback)
ISBN: 1-880410-22-2 (hardcover)
ISBN: 1-880410-25-7 (CD-ROM)

PMI Project Management Salary Survey – 2000 Edition

This 2000 Edition updates information first published in 1996 and expands coverage to over forty industry affiliations in nearly fifty countries in seven major geographic regions around the world. Its purpose is to establish normative compensation and benefits data for the project management profession on a global basis. The study provides salary, bonus/overtime, and deferred compensation information for specific job titles/positions within the project management profession. It also contains normative data for a comprehensive list of benefits and an array of other relevant parameters. *The PMI Project Management Salary Survey – 2000 Edition* is a vital new research tool for managers and HR professionals looking to retain or recruit employees, current members of the profession or those interested in joining it, researchers, and academics.

ISBN: 1-880410-26-5 (paperback)

Project Management for the Technical Professional

Michael Singer Dobson

Dobson, project management expert, popular seminar leader, and personality theorist, understands "promotion grief." He counsels those who prefer logical relationships to people skills and shows technical professionals how to successfully make the transition into management. This is a witty, supportive management primer for any "techie" invited to hop on the first rung of the corporate ladder. It includes self-assessment exercises; a skillful translation of general management theory and practice into tools, techniques, and systems that technical professionals will understand and accept; helpful "how to do it" sidebars; and action plans. It's also an insightful guide for those who manage technical professionals.

"The exercises and case studies featured here, along with the hands-on advice, hammer home fundamental principles. An intriguing complement to more traditional IT management guides, this is suitable for all libraries." —*Library Journal*

ISBN: 1-880410-76-1 (paperback)

The Project Surgeon: A Troubleshooter's Guide to Business Crisis Management

Boris Hornjak

A veteran of business recovery, project turnarounds and crisis prevention, Hornjak shares his "lessons learned" in this best practice primer for operational managers. He writes with a dual purpose—first for the practical manager thrust into a crisis situation with a mission to turn things around, make tough decisions under fire, address problems when they occur, and prevent them from happening again. Then his emphasis turns to crisis *prevention*, so you can free your best and brightest to focus on opportunities, instead of on troubleshooting problems, and ultimately break the failure/recovery cycle.

ISBN: 1-880410-75-3 (paperback)

Risk and Decision Analysis in Projects
Second Edition

John R. Schuyler

Schuyler, a consultant in project risk and economic decision analysis, helps project management professionals improve their decision-making skills and integrate them into daily problem solving. In this heavily illustrated second edition, he explains and demystifies key concepts and techniques, including expected value, optimal decision policy, decision trees, the value of information, Monte Carlo simulation, probabilistic techniques, modeling techniques, judgments and biases, utility and multi-criteria decisions, and stochastic variance.

ISBN: 1-880410-28-1 (paperback)

Earned Value Project Management
Second Edition

Quentin W. Fleming and Joel M. Koppelman

Now a classic treatment of the subject, this second edition updates this straightforward presentation of earned value as a useful method to measure actual project performance against planned costs and schedules throughout a project's life cycle. The authors describe the earned value concept in a simple manner so that it can be applied to any project, of any size, and in any industry. *Earned Value Project Management, Second Edition* may be the best-written, most easily understood project management book on the market today. Project managers will welcome this fresh translation of jargon into ordinary English. The authors have mastered a unique "early-warning" signal of impending cost problems in time for the project manager to react.

ISBN: 1880410-27-3 (paperback)

Project Management Experience and Knowledge Self-Assessment Manual

In 1999, PMI® completed a role delineation study for the Project Management Professional (PMP®) Certification Examination. A role delineation study identifies a profession's major performance domains (e.g., initiating the project or planning the project). It describes the tasks that are performed in each domain, and identifies the knowledge and skills that are required to complete the task. The role delineation task statements are presented in this manual in a format that enables you to assess how your project management experiences and training/education knowledge levels prepare you to complete each of the task statements. Individuals may use all of these tools to enhance understanding and application of PM knowledge to satisfy personal and professional career objectives. The self-assessment rating should not be used to predict, guarantee, or infer success or failure by individuals in their project management career, examinations, or related activities.

ISBN: 1-880410-24-9 (paperback)

Project Management Professional (PMP) Role Delineation Study

In 1999, PMI® completed a role delineation study for the Project Management Professional (PMP®) Certification Examination. In addition to being used to establish the test specifications for the examination, the study describes the tasks (competencies) PMPs perform and the project management knowledge and skills PMPs use to complete each task. Each of the study's tasks is linked to a performance domain (e.g., planning the project). Each task has three components to it: what the task is, why the task is performed, and how the task is completed. The *Role Delineation Study* is an excellent resource for educators, trainers, administrators, practitioners, and individuals interested in pursuing PMP certification.

ISBN: 1-880410-29-X (paperback)

PM 101 According to the Olde Curmudgeon

Francis M. Webster Jr.

Former editor-in-chief for PMI®, Francis M. Webster Jr. refers to himself as "the olde curmudgeon." The author, who has spent thirty years practicing, consulting on, writing about, and teaching project management, dispenses insider information to novice project managers with a friendly, arm-around-the-shoulder approach. He provides a history and description of all the components of modern project management; discusses the technical, administrative, and leadership skills needed by project managers; and details the basic knowledge and processes of project management, from scope management to work breakdown structure to project network diagrams. An excellent introduction for those interested in the profession themselves or in training others who are.

ISBN: 1-880410-55-9 (paperback)

The Project Sponsor Guide

Neil Love and Joan Brant-Love

This to-the-point and quick reading for today's busy executives and managers is a one-of-a-kind source that describes the unique and challenging support that executives and managers must provide to be effective sponsors of project teams. *The Project Sponsor Guide* is intended for executives and middle managers who will be, or are, sponsors of a project, particularly cross-functional projects. It is also helpful reading for facilitators and project leaders.

ISBN: 1-880410-15-X (paperback)

Don't Park Your Brain Outside: A Practical Guide to Improving Shareholder Value with SMART Management

Francis T. Hartman

Don't Park Your Brain Outside is the thinking person's guide to extraordinary project performance. Hartman has assembled a cohesive and balanced approach to highly effective project management. It is deceptively simple. Called SMART™, this new approach is Strategically Managed, Aligned, Regenerative, and Transitional. It is based on research and best practices, tempered by hard-won experience. SMART has saved significant time and money on the hundreds of large and small, simple and complex projects on which it has been tested. Are your projects SMART? Find out by reading this people-oriented project management book with an attitude!

ISBN: 1-880410-48-6 (hardcover)

The EnterPrize Organization: Organizing Software Projects for Accountability and Success

Neal Whitten

Neal Whitten is a twenty-three-year veteran of IBM and now president of his own consulting firm. Here he provides a practical guide to addressing a serious problem that has plagued the software industry since its beginning: how to effectively organize software projects to significantly increase their success rate. He proposes the "Enterprize Organization" as a model that takes advantage of the strengths of the functional organization, projectized organization, and matrix organization, while reducing or eliminating their weaknesses. The book collects the experiences and wisdom of thousands of people and hundreds of projects, and reduces *lessons learned* to a simple format that can be applied immediately to your projects.

ISBN: 1-880410-79-6 (paperback)

Teaming for Quality

H. David Shuster

Shuster believes most attempts at corporate cultural change die because people fail to realize how addicted they are to the way things are, the root causes of their resistance to change, and the degree to which their willingness to change depends on the moral philosophy of management. His new book offers a stimulating synthesis of classical philosophy, metaphysics, behavioral science, management theory and processes, and two decades of personal teaming experience to explain how individuals can choose change for themselves. Its philosophy-to-practice approach will help people team in ways that promote exceptionally high levels of bonding, individual creative expression (innovation), and collective agreement (consensus). Shuster shows how personal work fulfillment and corporate goals *can* work in alignment.

ISBN: 1-880410-63-X (paperback)

Project Management Software Survey

The PMI® *Project Management Software Survey* offers an efficient way to compare and contrast the capabilities of a wide variety of project management tools. More than two hundred software tools are listed with comprehensive information on systems features; how they perform time analysis, resource analysis, cost analysis, performance analysis, and cost reporting; and how they handle multiple projects, project tracking, charting, and much more. The survey is a valuable tool to help narrow the field when selecting the best project management tools.

ISBN: 1-880410-52-4 (paperback)
ISBN: 1-880410-59-1 (CD-ROM)

The Juggler's Guide to Managing Multiple Projects

Michael S. Dobson

This comprehensive book introduces and explains task-oriented, independent, and interdependent levels of project portfolios. It says that you must first have a strong foundation in time management and priority setting, then introduces the concept of Portfolio Management to timeline multiple projects, determine their resource requirements, and handle emergencies, putting you in charge for possibly the first time in your life!

ISBN: 1-880410-65-6 (paperback)

Recipes for Project Success

Al DeLucia and Jackie DeLucia

This book is destined to become "the" reference book for beginning project managers, particularly those who like to cook! Practical, logically developed project management concepts are offered in easily understood terms in a light-hearted manner. They are applied to the everyday task of cooking—from simple, single dishes, such as homemade tomato sauce for pasta, made from the bottom up, to increasingly complex dishes or meals for groups that in turn require an understanding of more complex project management terms and techniques. The transition between cooking and project management discussions is smooth, and tidbits of information provided with the recipes are interesting and humorous.

ISBN: 1-880410-58-3 (paperback)

Tools and Tips for Today's Project Manager

Ralph L. Kliem and Irwin S. Ludin

This guidebook is valuable for understanding project management and performing to quality standards. Includes project management concepts and terms—old and new—that are not only defined but also are explained in much greater detail than you would find in a typical glossary. Also included are tips on handling such seemingly simple everyday tasks as how to say "No" and how to avoid telephone tag. It's a reference you'll want to keep close at hand.

ISBN: 1-880410-61-3 (paperback)

The Future of Project Management

Developed by the 1998 PMI® Research Program Team and the futurist consultant firm of Coates and Jarratt, Inc., this guide to the future describes one hundred national and global trends and their implications for project management, both as a recognized profession and as a general management tool. It covers everything from knowbots, nanotechnology, and disintermediation to changing demography, information technology, social values, design, and markets.

ISBN: 1-880410-71-0 (paperback)

New Resources for PMP® Candidates

The following publications are resources that certification candidates can use to gain information on project management theory, principles, techniques, and procedures.

PMP Resource Package

The Cultural Dimension of International Business
by Gary P. Ferraro

Doing Business Internationally: The Guide to Cross-Cultural Success
by Terence Brake, Danielle Walker, Thomas Walker

Earned Value Project Management, Second Edition
by Quentin W. Fleming and Joel M. Koppelman

Effective Project Management: How to Plan, Manage, and Deliver Projects on Time and Within Budget
by Robert K. Wysocki, et al.

Focus Groups: A Step-by-Step Guide
by Gloria E. Bader and Catherine A. Rossi

Global Literacies: Lessons on Business Leadership and National Cultures
by Robert Rosen (Editor), Patricia Digh, Carl Phillips

A Guide to the Project Management Body of Knowledge (PMBOK® Guide) – 2000 Edition
by Project Management Institute

How to Lead Work Teams: Facilitation Skills, Second Edition
by Fran Rees

Human Resource Skills for the Project Manager
by Vijay K. Verma

The New Project Management
by J. Davidson Frame

Organizational Architecture: Designs for Changing Organizations
by David A. Nader, Marc S. Gerstein, Robert Shaw, and Associates

Principles of Project Management
by John Adams, et al.

Project & Program Risk Management
by R. Max Wideman, Editor

Project Management Experience and Knowledge Self-Assessment Manual
by Project Management Institute

Project Management: A Managerial Approach, Fourth Edition
by Jack R. Meredith and Samuel J. Mantel Jr.

Project Management: A Systems Approach to Planning, Scheduling, and Controlling, Seventh Edition
by Harold Kerzner

Visit PMI's website at *www.pmi.org*
or Shop at Our Online Bookstore at *www.pmibookstore.org*

Also Available from PMI

Project Management for Managers
Mihály Görög, Nigel J. Smith
ISBN: 1-880410-54-0 (paperback)

Project Leadership: From Theory to Practice
Jeffery K. Pinto, Peg Thoms, Jeffrey Trailer, Todd Palmer, Michele Govekar
ISBN: 1-880410-10-9 (paperback)

Annotated Bibliography of Project and Team Management
David I. Cleland, Gary Rafe, Jeffrey Mosher
ISBN: 1-880410-47-8 (paperback)
ISBN: 1-880410-57-5 (CD-ROM)

How to Turn Computer Problems into Competitive Advantage
Tom Ingram
ISBN: 1-880410-08-7 (paperback)

Achieving the Promise of Information Technology
Ralph B. Sackman
ISBN: 1-880410-03-6 (paperback)

Leadership Skills for Project Managers
Editors' Choice Series
Edited by Jeffrey K. Pinto, Jeffrey W. Trailer
ISBN: 1-880410-49-4 (paperback)

The Virtual Edge
Margery Mayer
ISBN: 1-880410-16-8 (paperback)

The ABCs of DPC
Edited by PMI's Design-Procurement-Construction Specific Interest Group
ISBN: 1-880410-07-9 (paperback)

Project Management Casebook
Edited by David I. Cleland, Karen M. Bursic, Richard Puerzer, A. Yaroslav Vlasak
ISBN: 1-880410-45-1 (paperback)

Project Management Casebook,
Instructor's Manual
Edited by David I. Cleland, Karen M. Bursic, Richard Puerzer, A. Yaroslav Vlasak
ISBN: 1-880410-18-4 (paperback)

The PMI Book of Project Management Forms
ISBN: 1-880410-31-1 (paperback)
ISBN: 1-880410-50-8 (diskette)

Principles of Project Management
John Adams et al.
ISBN: 1-880410-30-3 (paperback)

Organizing Projects for Success
Human Aspects of Project Management Series, Volume One
Vijay K. Verma
ISBN: 1-880410-40-0 (paperback)

Human Resource Skills for the Project Manager
Human Aspects of Project Management Series, Volume Two
Vijay K. Verma
ISBN: 1-880410-41-9 (paperback)

Managing the Project Team
Human Aspects of Project Management Series, Volume Three
Vijay K. Verma
ISBN: 1-880410-42-7 (paperback)

Value Management Practice
Michel Thiry
ISBN: 1-880410-14-1 (paperback)

The World's Greatest Project
Russell W. Darnall
ISBN: 1-880410-46-X (paperback)

Power & Politics in Project Management
Jeffrey K. Pinto
ISBN. 1-880410-43-5 (paperback)

Best Practices of Project Management Groups in Large Functional Organizations
Frank Toney, Ray Powers
ISBN: 1-880410-05-2 (paperback)

Project Management in Russia
Vladimir I. Voropajev
ISBN: 1-880410-02-8 (paperback)

A Framework for Project and Program Management Integration
R. Max Wideman
ISBN: 1-880410-01-X (paperback)

Quality Management for Projects & Programs
Lewis R. Ireland
ISBN: 1-880410-11-7 (paperback)

Project & Program Risk Management
Edited by R. Max Wideman
ISBN: 1-880410-06-0 (paperback)

The PMI Project Management Fact Book
ISBN: 1-880410-62-1 (paperback)

A Framework for Project Management
ISBN: 1-880410-82-6, Facilitator's Manual Set (3-ring binder)
ISBN: 1-880410-80-X, Participants' Manual Set, (paperback)

Order online at www.pmibookstore.org

Book Ordering Information

Phone: +412.741.6206

Fax: +412.741.0609

Email: pmiorders@abdintl.com

Mail: PMI Publications Fulfillment Center,
PO Box 1020, Sewickley, Pennsylvania 15143-1020 USA